Guests at an Ivory Tower

The Challenges Black Students Experience while Attending a Predominantly White University

Cherlyn A. Johnson

Foreword by Mary L. Rucker

UNIVERSITY PRESS OF AMERICA,® INC.
Lanham • Boulder • New York • Toronto • Oxford

Copyright © 2005 by
University Press of America,® Inc.
4501 Forbes Boulevard
Suite 200
Lanham, Maryland 20706
UPA Acquisitions Department (301) 459-3366

PO Box 317
Oxford
OX2 9RU, UK

Library of Congress Control Number: 2005928210
ISBN 0-7618-3183-5 (paperback : alk. ppr.)

Dedicated to I Am

Contents

Foreword

Over the course of her academic experience in the doctoral program at a pre-dominantly White private university, Cherlyn Johnson has articulated the experiences of African American students who perceive their social construction of reality of how things should be on an all-white college campus parallels that of the historic experiences of African Americans collectively. Her work has not only made a profound impact in the field of education, but it has also made a profound impact on the overall struggle for social equality and academic growth for African Americans in general.

Education is not a neutral process, and it should function as an instrument to facilitate the full integration of African Americans into the logic of the system or it should become the practice of freedom, a phenomenon, for everyone to think critically and creatively to participate in the transformation of a system (Hall, 1997)[1] that has catered to the interests of one group, the dominant group. No one is free until everyone is free. No one is equal until everyone is equal. No one is a victor until everyone is a victor. To believe that African Americans are revolutionary when they demand a fair education and to be treated with dignity is not some abstract phenomenon that is not easily discernable. African Americans like others are human beings with feelings, thoughts, expressions, values, and talents.

Many scholars have argued that African Americans like other people of color are an oppressed group. If they are oppressed, their oppression is experienced through the silence and avoidance of those who have the ability and power to assist them in their pursuit of academic development, achievement, and success. Research, however, indicates that African Americans are less

---

[1]See *Pedagogy of the Oppressed* by Paulo Freire, 1997.

likely to receive the same attention or assistance from their professors than their White counterparts. If African Americans received the same academic attention as White students, the racial and social gap in predominantly white institutions of higher learning would almost disappear.

Collective focus on African Americans' cognitive learning outcome in higher education could help close the gap between White and African American students' academic performance. However, what is missing in African American students' academic experiences is their full acceptance, integration, and participation into the social structure of the academy. That is, the structural conditions of predominantly white institutions of higher learning do not always provide the support network and human and social resources to help African American students achieve their goals. Cherlyn Johnson's book, *Guests at an Ivory Tower: The Challenges Black Students Experience while attending a Predominantly White University,* reminds me of a Scripture in the *Book of Daniel* that speaks to those in power of social institutions such as higher education that "You have been weighted in the balances, and found wanting" (Daniel, Chapter, 5:27). This message tells us that institutions of higher learning have been found wanting. If institutions of higher learning do not do more to address the critical issues with which African American and other minority students must confront on a daily basis, these institutions will eventually face serious consequences of disruption on their campuses. When students believe an institution is not interested in their academic success, they tend to drop out. However, Johnson addresses these very issues using Tinto's (1993) theory of student departure as the framework for her study and a study skills college course for the basis of her analysis. Johnson explains that Tinto's theory illustrates three phases of social and academic integration: separation, transition, and incorporation that are relevant to African American students' academic experiences at one particular predominantly white university. Johnson's book is not only helpful to African American students but also to professors who are interested in teaching under prepared students how to prepare academically.

By grappling with these complex issues, Johnson provides us with a lens through which we can view African American students' enrollment as no more than guests in an ivory tower. Johnson also illustrates how the study skills course, created by one of their senior professors, helps to "build the student's confidence in helping them to get control of their education." Johnson's book further allows us to hear African American students' suppressed voices as they discuss their academic experiences. Such illuminations reveal the historically low social status African Americans continue to experience in all forms of life in institutions of higher learning and in society. Moreover, Johnson's research echoes the work of many scholars such as that of Andrew

Hacker's *Two Nations: Black and White, Separate, Hostile, Unequal.* Her book offers us the meaning of race relevant to who gets access to what resources, particularly the human resources needed to help incorporate and socialize the marginalized into a system that has historically alienated them and treated them as the "elusive one."

For those educators who want to reshape their university cultures or transform the system that embraces every student regardless of race, class, and gender, and for those African American students who want to take upon themselves the struggle of becoming agents of their own educational outcome rather than staying objects and being avoided, Cherlyn Johnson's informative book will make a significant contribution to the field of education for reshaping university cultures and transforming the system.

Mary L. Rucker, Ph.D.

Preface

Remember the last time you were a guest at someone's house for the first time. How did they make you feel? Did they make you feel welcomed and comfortable? Did they engage in good conversations with you? Overall, were they delightful and gracious hosts or hostesses? When you left their house, did you want to return? If you answered yes to all of these questions then you became a part of a group in a new environment because of the actions of the hosts or hostesses. However, for some of you, the experience as a guest may not have been a good one. In fact, the experience was probably so appalling until you left early and vowed not to return. Perhaps, you "bit the bullet" and stayed.

The example above can be compared to how some Black students feel when they attend predominantly White universities today. With the many changes that have occurred over the years in higher education, Black students continue to have problems integrating socially and academically into these institutions. It has been suggested that if these students enrolled in a study skills course, it would assist them. However, the course was not always the solution to the problem.

In a year long study, I explored how Black students, who took a studies skills course, reported their social and academic experiences at a large predominantly white private university. I believed that it would be interesting to hear the strategies students used before and after taking a studies skills course. It was also important to hear the voices of these students as they struggled in an environment that, at times, was not always inviting.

Cherlyn A. Johnson, Ph.D.
Petersburg, Virginia
January 25, 2005

Acknowledgements

First and foremost, I want to thank and give the highest and greatest honor to God. He has given me guidance and wisdom throughout this project. Next, great appreciation and many thanks are extended to Dr. Susan Hynds, Dr. Marlene Blumin, Dr. Donald Leu and the late Dr. Peter Mosenthal for being wonderful and wise professors.

In addition, much gratitude is given to Dr. Ethel S. Robinson and Dr. Christine Hoskins for their words of encouragement while I completed this project. Moreover, I want to thank the students in this study who let me hear their voices as they pursued their education in an institution of higher learning. Last but not least, I want to honor my parents, Rev. Dr. and Mrs. Isadore Johnson, Sr. and family.

Chapter One

Introduction

Latrice, a Black female, is a first semester freshman at a large, predominantly White private university in the northeast. Coming to this university has been a culture shock for her since she has attended an all Black high school located in the inner city. Nevertheless, she is determined to fulfill her dreams of becoming an attorney. She decides to take 15 credit hours of course work that include Biology/Biology lab, Writing Interpretation, Probability and Statistics, Introduction to French, and African Dance. Latrice is pleased with her courses and schedule, especially since she also has work study.

However, after two weeks into the semester, she realizes that college is not like high school. In high school, she could study and do homework assignments the night before and still get good grades. Furthermore, her teachers knew her parents and her older siblings. Some of her teachers even worshipped at the same church with her.

Now, as a college student, her situation is different. She has become overwhelmed by the amount of reading and writing assignments she has to complete before the next class. She is also struggling in Probability and Statistics. Biology lab is taking about six hours to complete because she has to listen to tapes. In large lectures, she feels more like a "number" rather than an individual. Moreover, unlike high school where she felt more comfortable approaching her teachers, she is unable to do so with her professors. The reason she believes her White professors are unapproachable is that they appear intimidating and lack a real interest in establishing rapport with the students. In addition, she is homesick, feels isolated, and is very lonely. She remembers seeing an advertisement in the student class-scheduling handbook about a study skills course. She decides to add that course to her schedule. She hopes that this course will help because she really wants to do well her first semester in college.

"Latrice," though not an actual informant for this study, is a composite portrayal of the personal characteristics and circumstances typical of students who sought out study skills courses in the university where this study took place. This research project focused on a group of Black students who took one of the study skills courses at a large, predominantly White private university in the northeast. It is important to study students like Latrice because, even though Black students take study skills courses, few studies focus on the extent to which these students perceive study skills courses as being instrumental to their social and academic integration into a predominantly White institutional environment. To this end, this study focused on the following questions:

1. How do Black students who take study skills courses perceive their initial experiences at a predominantly White private institution, when compared with their previous school experiences?
2. What strategies and techniques do students talk about using prior to taking a study skills course?
3. What role, if any, do the study skills courses appear to play in these students' social and academic integration into a predominantly White private institution?

1.1 PURPOSE OF THE STUDY

Statistics show that the number of Black students attending colleges and universities is at an all time high: "More than 1.4 million black students are currently enrolled in higher education" (Cross & Slater, 1997, p. 86). These students now "make up 10.3 percent of all students enrolled in higher education" (Cross & Slater, 1997, p. 86). Researchers also explain that about eight in ten Black students attend predominantly White colleges and universities, and this large proportion of Black students attending these institutions may continue into the future (Feagin, Vera, & Imani, 1996).

Despite the large number of Black students seeking college diplomas, compared to White students at predominantly White institutions, they take longer to finish (Allen, 1988; Braddock & McPartland, 1988) and drop out more often (Allen, 1988; Love, 1993; McCauley, 1988; Walters, 1996), usually by the end of their second year of college (Allen, 1988). Allen (1988) argues, in his study, that Black students are three times as likely to leave college at the end of their sophomore year for academic reasons when compared to the total predominantly White university population. More than half of these Black students have left for nonacademic reasons (Allen, 1988).

In general, 1997/1998 statistics illustrate that "only 37 percent of all blacks entering college graduate from the same institution within six years" (Cross & Slater, 1997, p. 86). On the contrary, "the graduation rate for white students is 59 percent" (p. 86). The low graduation rate among Black college students at predominantly White universities has been linked, in part, to these students being academically underprepared (Allen, 1988; Jacobi, 1991; O'Brien, 1989; Pounds, 1987; Slater, 1995; Tinto, 1987; Tinto, 1993; Wright, 1987). They also have faced or encountered psychosocial barriers such as isolation, loneliness, alienation, racism, and environmental dissatisfaction (Allen, 1987; Allen, 1992; Bello-Ogunu, 1997; Fleming, 1984; Love, 1993; Nottingham, Rosen & Parks, 1992; Phelon-Rucker, 2000; Philip, 1993; Turner, 1994; Willie & McCord, 1972) at these institutions.

In sum, when compared to their White counterparts, Black students have had more difficulties finishing their college degree programs, if they do at all. One explanation for the failure of colleges and universities to retain Black students is because of the disjuncture between their prior educational institutions and the predominantly White institutions, and they are not able to integrate successfully into the academic mainstream (Allen, 1988; Love, 1993; Richardson, Simmons, & Santos, 1987; Tinto, 1987; Tinto, 1993).

In light of this problem, colleges and universities have devised ways to retain minority students. One way has been through study skills courses (Giles-Gee, 1989; Spitzberg & Thorndike, 1992; Townsend, 1994). Research in this area shows the general benefits and measures of taking a study skills course in terms of outcome measures such as grade point average, social networks, and retention statistics (Giles-Gee, 1989; Spitzberg & Thorndike, 1992; Townsend, 1994). However, few studies have focused on the perceptions of Black students who take these courses.

Despite a few encouraging studies on the overall benefits of study skills courses, the attrition rate (Allen, 1988, Braddock & McPartland, 1988) and time of completion (Allen, 1988; Braddock & McPartland, 1988; Cross & Slater, 1997) for Black students at predominantly White private institutions are still alarmingly high when compared to White students. Few studies, if any, have explored the perceptions of Black students who enroll in study skills courses in terms of their social and academic integration. To that end, this study focuses on a group of Black students who have taken a study skills course at a large, predominantly White private institution in the northeast. More specifically, this study explores their perceptions of the social and academic difficulties they have faced at this predominantly White private university when compared with their previous schooling. It is important to obtain these students' perceptions so that we could have the opportunity to hear how they report their academic and social experiences at this predominantly White private university. It is also pertinent that these Black students' perceptions be obtained on their previous schooling experiences because this information can show the type of learning environment they are leaving as they matriculate into the university. Last, acquiring data on how these students talk about the learning strategies they used before and after taking a study skills course could show whether the course played a role in their academic and social integration.

The information in this study could be particularly useful to university administrators, program directors, practitioners, policy makers, and researchers. As mentioned previously, 80 percent of Black students attend predominantly White institutions where there is likely to be a disjuncture between their secondary and the post secondary school experiences. Therefore, university administrators interested in the retention and integration of these students could come to know and understand the academic and social obstacles these particular students face as they attempt to integrate into a predominantly White campus environment. Understanding the difficulties these students face as they pursue their academic careers could help administrators establish policies, procedures, and practices for retention. Since study skills courses have been touted as one way for colleges and universities to assist and retain some of these students, this research could offer program directors and practitioners with a better understanding of how to improve and develop these courses and programs to help Black students in their academic and social integration. On the level of public policy, this research could provide information pertinent to the specific educational needs of Black college students.

Finally, although there have been numerous studies on the process of integration into colleges and universities (Allen, 1987; Allen, 1992; Bello-Ogunu, 1997; Feagin, Vera & Imani, 1996; Fleming, 1984; Nottingham, Rosen & Parks, 1992; Philip, 1993; Tinto, 1987; Tinto, 1993; Turner, 1994) and although much research has focused on the general benefits of study skills programs in the retention process (Blanc, Debuhr & Martin, 1983; Bender, 1997; Bruno, 1990; Fidler & Hunter, 1989; Gebelt, Parilis, Kramer & Wilson, 1996; Giles-Gee, 1989; Reis, 1989; Spitzberg & Thorndike, 1992; Stupka, 1993; Townsend, 1994), few recent studies have focused on the unique needs and perspectives of Black students who enroll in these courses. Such research could add to our current understanding of the role of study skills programs in the integration and retention of Black students with the university community.

The following literature review presents issues that pertain to the education of Black students in higher education and addresses the relatively scarce information about Black students who take study skills courses at predominantly White institutions. In addition, the literature review presents the development and effectiveness of study skills courses generally and, more specifically, discusses how these courses benefit Black students.

1.2 REVIEW OF THE LITERATURE

A. Integrating Into the Academic Mainstream:
The Challenges for Black Students

Even though there are a number of ethnic groups and women attending predominantly White institutions (PWIs) today, many of these institutions have been originally designed for White, Christian males (Levine, 1989). Thus, the policies, practices, and procedures established have excluded ethnic groups such as blacks from this structure (Love, 1993). Therefore, it is not strange that blacks feel and are treated like "guests" at predominantly White universities (Feagin, Vera, & Imani, 1996; Turner, 1994) and "left to fend for themselves" (Townsend, 1994, p. 85) once admitted into these institutions. Love (1993) also states that Black students experience cultural dissonance or a "gap between the culture the students bring with them to college and the institutional culture they find in PWIs" (p. 30).

In general, Tinto's theory of student departure (Tinto, 1993) illustrates the integration of all students into the academic and social systems of an institution or the "movement of individuals from membership in one group to that in another" (p. 92). Tinto has applied Van Gennep's (1960/1909) framework, which discusses the rites of passage in tribal societies, to present his theory. He points out that students are typically integrated into these systems through the stages of "separation," "transition," and "incorporation." Separation requires students to "disassociate themselves, in varying degrees, from membership in the communities of the past, most typically those associated with the family, the local high school, and local areas of residence" (Tinto, 1993, p. 95). With the stage of transition, students must make the "passage between the old and the new, before the full adoption of new norms and patterns of behavior and after the onset of separation from old ones"(p. 97). In the final stage, incorporation, students are challenged to find and adopt the norms and behavioral patterns appropriate to their colleges or universities (Tinto, 1993). Tinto (1993) also points out that these stages are not always clearly sequenced. That is, they can occur partially, overlap and be repeated (Tinto, 1993).

For Black students arriving on predominantly White university campuses, the separation stage can be even more challenging than for their White counterparts. D'Augelli and Hashberger (1993) affirm in their study that when African-American students arrive on campus, they know fewer students than do their White peers and do not have the advantage of an automatic social support system. Many African-American students also come from high schools and communities where they are the majority and where their academic backgrounds are similar to the other African American students (D'Augelli & Hashberger, 1993). However, the researchers state that once on campus, the students become a "distinct minority" (D'Augelli & Hashberger, 1993, p. 68).

A number of studies also have demonstrated that a large number of Black students come to college academically underprepared due to understaffed and ill-equipped inner city public schools (Allen, 1988; Jacobi, 1991; O'Brien, 1989; Pounds, 1987; Slater, 1995; Wright, 1987). Hale (1994) points out that the causes for these problems are a reflection of the inequality of school financing. She cites Jonathan Kozol to explain the "disparity in funding of wealthy suburban school districts in comparison to poor city school districts" (p. 123):

> The richer districts—those in which the property lots and houses are more highly valued—have more revenue, derived from taxing land and homes, to fund their public schools. The reputation of the schools, in turn, adds to the value of their homes, and this, in turn, expands the tax base for their public schools. The fact that they can levy lower taxes than the poorer districts, but exact more money, raises values even more; and this, again, means further funds for smaller classes and for higher teacher salaries within the public schools (p. 125).

This situation may explain why minority parents believe that their children's education is inferior to that of Caucasian children in affluent suburbs (Ogbu, 1995).

Research further demonstrates that inner city high schools lack the course offerings and competitive and motivational environments needed for minority students to succeed in a four-year college program (Richardson, Simmons, & Santos, 1987). Black students, in particular, are often placed in "vocational courses or tracks that do not lead to college and with teachers who have lower expectations for their academic achievement" (Thomas & Hirsch, 1989, p.65). According to Hynds (1997), students who are placed in the lower tracks often become disenchanted with school. Citing Ogbu (1995), she points out that Black students are underrepresented in the higher-level courses. Ogbu (1995) argues:

> Many involuntary minority students such as black students, for example, often avoid taking advanced-level science, math and foreign language courses because they often do not see other black students in such classes. This situation has given rise, in many areas of the United States, to a misconception among many black students that advanced-level mathematics, science, and foreign language courses are too difficult for black students and should be avoided (p. 97).

While schools are unequal in fundamental ways, primarily Black schools can provide a nurturing and supportive environment for Black students that encourage and empower these students to enjoy learning. As hooks (1994) observes from her experience of attending an all-Black high school:

> They (teachers) were committed to nurturing intellect so that we could become scholars, thinkers, and cultural workers—black folks who used our "minds" . . . . My teachers were on a mission. To fulfill that mission, my teachers made sure they "knew" us. They knew our parents, our economic status, where we worshipped, what our homes were like, and how we were treated in the family . . . . Attending school was sheer joy. I loved being a student. I loved learning (pp. 2-4).

Unfortunately, the solidarity that Black students' experience in an all Black learning environment often leads to a disjuncture in the academic mainstream once they move into higher education. Findings cited from a national study showed that students who attended predominantly Black high schools were not prepared for the reality of being a racial minority at predominantly White institutions (Allen, 1988).

The transition to campus life for Black students at predominantly White universities can often be stressful (Smedley, Hector, & Harrell, 1993) and unwelcoming (Love, 1993; Mack, Tucker, Archulata, Degroot, Hernandez, & Cha, 1997; Malaney & Shively, 1995). Smedley, Hector, and Harrell (1993) contend that there are two forms of stress that have been identified among Black students: psychosocial stress and minority-status stress. Not surprisingly, for Black students, psychosocial stress (i.e., isolation, loneliness, alienation, racism, environmental dissatisfaction, etc.) has occurred more on predominantly White campuses than on predominantly Black campuses (Allen, 1987; Allen, 1992; Bello-Ogunu, 1997; Fleming, 1984; Love, 1993; Nottingham, Rosen, & Parks, 1992; Phelon-Rucker, 2000; Turner, 1994; Willie & McCord, 1972). Furthermore, it has been found that the pressures contributing to minority-status stress among all minority students pertains to concerns about:

> their academic preparedness, questions about their legitimacy as students at the university, perceptions of negative expectations from white peers and from the faculty, and concerns over parental/family expectations and lack of understanding of the peculiar demands of attending a highly competitive university (Smedley, Hector, & Harrell, 1993, p. 447).

Moreover, despite individual accomplishments, minorities are stigmatized for being perceived as recipients of affirmative action decisions (Feagin, Vera, & Imani, 1996; Smedley, Hector, & Harrell, 1993). In general, Smedley et al. (1993) show that African-American freshmen students have greater minority-status stress than do other minority freshmen.

Another stressful barrier is that "many black students complete an entire academic year without ever taking a class under a black professor, or even seeing one on campus" (Bello-Ogunu, 1997, p. 11). Bello-Ogunu (1997) points out that most predominantly White institutions do not have many Black faculty or administrators, and this often leads Black students to be left without Black mentors or role models. He further attests that the Blacks they see while pursuing their education at predominantly White institutions usually are janitors, clerical workers, or coaches (Bello-Ogunu, 1997). Moreover, many Black students begin and complete their academic career by being the only Black student in most of their courses (Bello-Ogunu, 1997).

Allen (1992) points out even more barriers or inequalities that exist within the university system. He posits that

> among these barriers are admissions requirements that rely heavily on culturally and economically biased standardized tests; faculties dominated by middle class, White males; soaring costs accompanied by inadequate financial aid programs; destructive pedagogical styles that emphasize "dog eat dog" competition; the embrace of exclusionary ethics that undercut attempts to achieve cultural pluralism and diversity; and norms that elevate "sorting out" procedures over approaches that emphasize student learning, such as value-added, remedial strategies (p. 42).

In addition, Fleming (1984) explains that Black males receive little support on predominantly White university campuses as compared to predominantly Black university campuses. Nevertheless, when Black males are academically integrated into the predominantly White institution, they perform better than Black males who are not academically integrated at majority institutions (Davis, 1994). In Fleming's study, Black females, on the other hand, are more socially assertive, articulate, and outspoken on predominantly White campuses than on predominantly Black campuses (Fleming, 1983; Fleming, 1984). This characteristic emanates from the "'matriarchal or strong and dominant stereotype" that these women have possessed since the ending of slavery (Fleming, 1983, p.51). Moreover, the reason these women tend to portray this matriarchal image more on predominantly White college campuses than on Black campuses is because there are fewer Black males to please (Fleming, 1984). However, Fleming states that being assertive comes with the price of being ostracized on predominantly White campuses.

Another degrading experience that challenged Black students is the stereotypical images held by Whites at predominantly White institutions. A study conducted by Feagin, Vera, and Imani (1996) shows that Blacks are often perceived as being good in certain sports like basketball. Inside the classroom, the researchers point out that Black students have to contend with the stereotypical comments and actions of White faculty. The study also maintains that when parties are given on the predominantly White campus, the primarily White university employees exhibit differential treatment toward whites versus blacks (Feagin, Vera, & Imani, 1996). Apparently, the university staff views black parties "as more of a serious disturbance or security risk than the white student parties" (Feagin, Vera, & Imani, 1996, p.125).

Attending these predominantly White universities may often reinforce "double consciousness" among Black individuals as they pursue their education. Dubois (1989, Original Edition, 1903) identifies double consciousness as:

> this sense of always looking at one's self through the eyes of others, of measuring one's soul by the tape of a world that looks on in amused contempt and pity. One ever feels his twoness—an American, a Negro; two souls, two thoughts, two unreconciled strivings; two warring ideals in one dark body, whose dogged strength alone keeps it from being torn asunder (p. 5).

In contrast to the Black college experience, the experiences of Caucasian students are very different in the sense that they "do not experience [problems with] acculturation, at least not, to the degree that minority students do" (Wright, 1987, p.11). Padilla, Trevino, Gonzalez, and Trevino (1997), who cite several researchers, stress that Caucasian students have a support system within the university and society where they can "successfully confront the many challenges of college life" (p. 133). That is, they have professors, students, staff, and administrators of the same racial group who can serve as role models (Padilla et al, 1997). Caucasian students also have "greater cultural continuity between the home and college environment that provides them with a sense of familiarity and security" (p. 133). Moreover, it is most likely that they have had someone in their family who has attended college and, therefore, can help them with the transition to college (Padilla et al, 1997).

In the area of finance, Caucasians are "nearly four times as likely to earn the higher incomes necessary to pay the sharply increasing costs of higher education" (Cross & Slater, 1997, p. 80). The researchers stress that in 1995, "more than 5.7 million white families had incomes above $100,000 in comparison to only 224,000 Black families of the same income level" (p. 80). In short, reasons ranging from "financial and academic to feelings of isolation and alienation" have been why Black students left or dropped out of predominantly White institutions before obtaining their degrees (Philip, 1993, p. 26).

In order to retain Black students, several researchers have suggested that colleges and universities should provide learning assistance and skill development opportunities for assisting them in their academic achievement (Green 1989; Pounds, 1987; Pounds, 1989; Rowser, 1997; Willie & McCord 1972). Pounds (1989) argues that having such assistance will give Black students the desire to remain and complete their studies in college. In response to the call, predominantly White institutions have established various programs to retain these students (Clark & Crawford, 1992; Lewis, 1986; Love, 1993; O'Brien, 1989; Townsend, 1994). One very common approach toward facilitating student retention has been through study skills courses. The next section presents the development and effectiveness of study skills programs generally and, more specifically, how these courses benefit Black students.

B. The Development and Effectiveness of Study Skills Programs

Because of inadequate academic preparation among students, basic skills programs have grown enormously in the past years (Spitzberg & Thorndike, 1992). However, study skills programs, or "success" courses, should not be viewed only as a twentieth-century creation (Stupka, 1988). Stupka (1988) states that they were first offered in 1888 at Boston College. In 1911, Reed College in Portland, Oregon, offered such a course for academic credit. He notes that years later after enrollments into colleges began to increase and then decrease in the 1970s and "retention became the new buzz word," a renewed interest developed which led to the student "success" courses (p. 3). For the purpose of this review, the terms "study skills courses" and "success" courses will be used interchangeably since they are often indistinguishable from each other.

It should be made clear that colleges and universities are not only offering study skills programs or "success" courses to students who are underrepresented in higher education but also to athletes, physically handicapped, and honor students (Stupka, 1988). In fact, it has been argued that no student should be exempted from taking a study skills course. A study conducted by Sheridan (1982) demonstrates that the study skills of probationary freshmen are often as deficient as those of the average freshmen. Thus, she concludes the need for study skills classes for all students. Moreover, she states that having a study skills program is a critical factor for student retention in the university.

For students, many study skills courses and programs are premised on the notion of teaching them how to become self-regulated learners (Pintrich, 1995). Self-regulated learning "involves the active, goal-directed, self control of behavior, motivation, and cognition for academic tasks by an individual student" (p. 5). Pintrich states that self-regulated learning allows students to learn through experience and self-reflection as they approach academic tasks. Socially, researchers have affirmed that these study skills programs have created learning communities within the college or university (Spitzberg & Thorndike, 1992).

Research revealed that these courses were generally beneficial for students who enrolled in them. Stupka (1993) illustrated in his seven-semester study that students who took the student success course on academic performance and persistence were more successful than those who did not take the course. That is, students in the course completed more credits and dropped out less often than those not enrolled in the course. Similarly, a study by Reis (1989) maintained that students who took the "College Success" course had higher GPAs and a higher retention rate than those not enrolled in the course. Moreover, a large proportion of these students were first-time students (Reis, 1989). Students who took the "College Success" course at Columbia College in California also showed improvements in grades and units that were completed and attempted (Bruno, 1990).

Study skills components were also included in many programs to assist students in academia. For example, the freshmen seminar, University 101, at the University of South Carolina offered credit courses to students that ranged from study skills to better interaction with faculty (Jewler, 1989). Studies showed that students who took the seminar had a higher graduation rate and sophomore retention had increased (Fidler & Hunter, 1989). Likewise, at another institution, a Supplemental Instruction Program (SI) that provided students with help in reading, reasoning, and study skills enabled those enrolled to receive higher GPAs and course grades (Blanc, Debuhr, & Martin, 1983). In addition, the students withdrew less often than those not enrolled in the program (Blanc, Debuhr, & Martin, 1983). A study of undergraduate students in the Gateway Psychology Program at Rutgers University showed that participants in this program were "being retained at a rate comparable to the university at large" (Gebelt, Parilis, Kramer, & Wilson, 1996, p.10). Even though these students took more than four years to complete college, the program did provide them with the needed study skills to graduate (Gebelt et al., 1996).

The effects of combining a study skills course with tutoring were also found beneficial. At Penn State, students who enrolled in the comprehensive College Skills Development Program, which consisted of a combined study skills course and required tutoring sessions, did better academically than students who only took the study skills course (Bender, 1997). In short, according to Stupka (1988), study skills programs and "success" courses "increase the students' awareness of the power they have over their lives" (p.5). In addition, they help students become "independent learners" (p.7) or "masters of their own learning" (Zimmerman, 1990, p.4).

While research has demonstrated the overall benefits of study skills courses and programs, only a few studies have explored the benefits for Black students. A study conducted by Giles-Gee (1989) showed that Black freshmen students who participated in a retention-related project that stressed academic advising, study skills training, and the use of services improved their grades significantly after one year compared to previous students who did not have the benefit of the project. Black students who enrolled in the freshmen seminar, University 101, at the University of South Carolina had "higher sophomore retention rates than whites—as high as 87.2 percent—in every year from 1974 to 1992" (Townsend, 1994, p.87). In addition, the program included seminars on African-American culture and history (Townsend, 1994). Socially, these programs benefited minority students. For example, a program at an elite western university gave minority students the opportunity to study together and establish support systems of learning (Spitzberg & Thorndike, 1992). Spitzberg and Thorndike (1992) emphasized those successful minority students who remained at universities often "relied on the supportive environment of the basic skills program to help them succeed in the academic mainstream" (p.117). Moreover, for Black students, being successful in their studies would be the basis or a contributing factor for increasing their self-esteem (Steele, 1991).

In sum, we know from previous research that Black students experience a disconnection between their high school environments and that of a university mainstream environment. We also know that they have experiences that prevent their integration at predominantly White universities. Last, research indicates that these students are not graduating at a rate as high as Whites at these institutions. Therefore, to decrease attrition, universities have established retention programs.

Study skills courses have been suggested as one means of supporting the retention of these students. The few studies that do focus on the benefit of study skills courses for Black students pertain to outcome measures such as grade point average, retention, and the development of social networks. There are not any current studies that have explored students' perceptions of study skills courses, particularly as related to their academic and social integration into the academic mainstream. While research on the general benefits of study skills programs are useful, they offer little information to administrators, practitioners, and researchers in terms of how the students report implementing the study strategies in their academic and social lives. To that end, this study focuses on how a group of Black students, who have taken a study skills course, perceive their initial academic and social experiences at this predominantly White private university when compared to their earlier schooling experience. Moreover, the study gives insight on which techniques or strategies these students talked about using before and after taking a study skills course.

Chapter Two

Methodology

To establish a foundation for this study, I begin by describing the theoretical framework I used while conducting this research. Next, I discuss the procedures for selecting informants, collecting and analyzing the data. I also present my background and assumptions as an African-American graduate student, an instructor of study skills, and a researcher at the university where this study took place. I then introduce each student in the study. Finally, I discuss the history, characteristics, and perceived benefits of the study skills courses at this predominantly White private university (PWPI or PWI).

2.1 THEORETICAL FRAMEWORK

Tinto's (1993) theory of student departure was the framework for this qualitative study. Using Van Gennep's (1960/1909) framework, which describes the rites of passage in tribal societies, Tinto's theory illustrated the three phases of social and academic integration: separation, transition, and incorporation. This study used Tinto's theory to analyze the perceptions of a group of Black students who had taken a study skills course in terms of their academic and social integration into a PWPI.

Typically, Tinto's theory illustrated the integration of all students into the social and academic systems of an institution. Specifically presenting Black students' perceptions of their academic and social experiences at a PWPI would enrich the theory. That is, we would come to understand these students' levels of emotions and thoughts as they entered and moved through this university. Moreover, we would come to know if the study skills courses aided the students in their social and academic integration once completed. By interviewing and exploring these students' perceptions, I was able to analyze their responses and returned for subsequent interviews with questions that emerged from the analysis to determine their academic and social integration into the institution.

2.2 PROCEDURE FOR SELECTING STUDENTS

Students were selected through purposeful sampling (Bogdan and Biklen, 1992). With purposeful sampling, the researcher also chooses "particular subjects to include because they are believed to facilitate the expansion" of the theory (p.71). I selected Black students formerly enrolled in study skills courses. All of the students were former students with the exception of one. This particular student was an undergraduate teaching assistant (UTA) for one of the study skills courses. I contacted 11 students by letter. I waited two weeks and then sent a follow-up letter. However, I did not receive a large response from the students, particularly Black males.

Therefore, I called and e-mailed the students to find out why they did not want to participate. Apparently, the students had a problem with the part of the letter that said they would have to keep a journal about their experiences. Because I was in danger of losing these students, I decided to exclude the journals from the study. Although nine students responded and agreed to participate after I excluded the journals, one student had to leave the university during the fall semester due to an illness. Thus, I was left with eight students, four males and four females. Because I had difficulties finding other participants to fit my criteria, I was not able to seek out additional participants when data saturation began to occur with this particular group. Nevertheless, as themes and patterns began to emerge, I scheduled subsequent interviews with participants, seeking out negative instances of the phenomena that emerged from my data. At the study's inception, all of the students had completed the courses and grades had been submitted.

2.3 DATA COLLECTION

I explored the academic and social world of each participant by compiling data through in-depth one-on-one, audiotaped interviews. The interviews were done in my cubicle in the department where I worked and the study rooms of the main library of the university. The few interviews conducted in my cubicle were done only on Friday mornings when there were not many people within the vicinity. In addition, I conducted audiotaped interviews with the director/professor of the study skills courses in her office. By interviewing the director/professor, I was able to obtain information on the history of the courses and the professor's perceptions of the courses' benefits to the students. The interviewing process allowed a "conversation with a purpose" (Merriam, 1988, p. 71) to occur with the students and the director/professor. Interviewing the participants and the director/professor was also pertinent because, as Patton (1980) argues,

> We cannot observe how people have organized the world and the meanings they attach to what goes on in the world—we have to ask people questions about those things. The purpose of interviewing, 'then, is to allow us to enter into the other person's perspective' (p.196).

The one-hour in-depth interviews were semi-structured. Less structured interviews allowed the participants to "define the world in unique ways" (Merriam, 1988, p. 73). The interviews were also conducted in two phases. The first phase of the interview questions focused on the students' background, high school experience and academic and social experiences freshman year at the university (see Appendix). The second phase of the interview questions dealt with the students' academic and social experiences after taking a study skills course (see Appendix).

While I conducted the interviews, I took notes and wrote questions that arose during the conversations. Writing down questions helped me to ask and clarify information the students provided at that time. In addition, this procedure allowed me to avoid interrupting the flow of the students' thoughts. After each interview, I transcribed the conversations verbatim. I also read, made notes, and posed questions in the margins of the transcripts next to the students' passages. This technique not only enabled me to ask questions at the follow-up interviews, but it also helped me to keep a running list of themes as they developed. In addition, analytic memos were written to help maintain a focus on emerging themes.

The interview transcripts were cross-checked by the participants and the director/ professor of the study skills courses. This procedure allowed the participants and the director/professor to read and clarify excerpts from the transcripts in subsequent interviews. I also read excerpts to the participants during the interviews. The participants were interviewed up to six times until the data became redundant or saturated (Bodgan & Biklen, 1992). The transcripts amounted to approximately 500 pages.

2.4 DATA ANALYSIS

My data analysis was an ongoing process from the inception to the conclusion of the study. Analytic induction, which is an approach for collecting and analyzing data in qualitative research, was used in this study (Bodgan & Biklen, 1992). With analytic induction, I concentrated on selecting examples of negative cases of the phenomena as they emerged from my ongoing analysis (Bodgan & Biklen, 1992).

Although Tinto's (1993) stages of integration formed an overriding framework or a lens for analyzing the data, I discovered themes that arose within this framework for these participants. Therefore, I created concept maps of these themes from a running list I composed as I read the interviews. I also used the concept maps to help me write memos.

After all the interviews were completed, I reread my memos, transcripts, and concept maps. Because this aspect of the analysis became more intense, I decided to create two charts illustrating the themes found in each phase of the interviews. The charts were labeled as Phase I and Phase II. I then created a column for the academic themes and the social themes for each chart. The students' names along with the page numbers where the passages were found were written under the themes. While I analyzed each chart, I began combining similar themes under major themes as my understanding of the students' experiences became clearer. Later, I excerpted selected passages from the interview transcripts on the computer and placed them into computer files under specific themes.

2.5 LIMITATIONS OF STUDY

This study only explored the perceptions of eight Black students after they took a study skills course at a predominantly White private university. Students were not interviewed before or while enrolled in an SSC course. Therefore, this research cannot be generalized to the experiences of all Black students or students of other ethnic groups who take study skills courses at predominantly White institutions. However, (1) grades had been given, and (2) questions focused on each student's experience in a predominantly White private institution and the study strategies they reported using before and after taking a study skills course, not on the degree to which they felt the course was beneficial.

Because a majority of the students in this study were my former students, I also had established rapport with the students prior to the interviews. Having established this prior rapport appeared to have made it easier for these students to talk about their experiences, and they returned each time for follow-up interviews. Moreover, since race is a "thorny" topic, I felt more comfortable getting information from students I knew. By doing so, I believed I would get the richest, most valid data from these students.

Nevertheless, it could be argued that the former students may have tried to please me with their responses to my questions. Next, because the students and I were Black, it could be argued that the issue of race may have been more salient in the conversations than it would have been if I had not been the same race as my participants. Nonetheless, in any case, I tried to explore other issues besides race in their experiences at the university.

In the next section, I present my background and assumptions as an African-American graduate student, an instructor of the study skills courses, and a researcher at this PWPI. In addition, I introduce my participants for this study and give information about the study skills courses at this institution.

2.6 RESEARCH SITE AND RESPONDENTS

A. Background

I really liked it (Big-Time University)[1]. . . . I thought the people were very friendly. At first, I thought they were acting or pretending just because they wanted me to apply . . . accept their offer. But then they were really concerned you know. Like this is the place I want to be. . . I loved it, the surrounding, everything. And to see all these trees! People use to make fun of me because I would see the [other] birds [and] not pigeons fly around. And the trees, I mean green [grass]. . . . I was just like wow!

Kenya, Junior, from New York City

When I first arrived on the campus of Big-Time University (BTU), I too was taken or impressed with the beauty of its surroundings and the friendliness of its people. I was proud of my decision to come to this beautiful academic institution. While the green trees and the different types of birds captured Kenya's eyes, it was the tall, stately buildings representing great prestige and honor that captivated me. These buildings, which were a mixture of old and new architecture, encircled a central area known on campus as "the quad." On the well-cut green lawns were tall trees that lined walkways in this quadrangle. Known as the "school on the hill," BTU sits on two hundred acres of land that is surrounded by stores, restaurants, a hotel, a small shopping mall, and residential neighborhoods. For the academic year of 1998/1999, 12,130 undergraduate students attended this "student-centered research university"; 905 were African-American and 9,739 were White ([BTU] "Facts and Figures").

---

[1]Names used for individuals, programs, and institutions in this study are pseudonyms.

Another positive aspect of attending BTU was the small department where I would spend the next few years of my doctoral work. I was proud to be in this department because I felt welcomed, and I immediately became a part of a growing family. From the conversations and relationships I quickly developed with the professors, I knew the support I needed would be there. That is, from the beginning to the completion of my doctoral program, these professors did not ignore or view any of my academic concerns or interests as petty. Instead, we kept open lines of communication and discussed my academic concerns and interests. They also insisted that I address them by their first names. This not only amazed me but also helped convince me that I was definitely a part of an academic family and not just another "number."

However, as I became more involved with the study skills courses, I noticed that my amiable experience as an African-American female doctoral student and the experiences of the Black undergraduate students at this university were not the same. While I was able to develop relationships with my professors, some of these undergraduate students were afraid to talk to their professors. Moreover, these students expressed how the large lectures made them feel more like numbers rather than individuals. Thus, I began to wonder, what happened after Black undergraduate students arrived on this campus? Specifically, what happened to enthusiastic students like Kenya? Did that enthusiasm remain or change? If that enthusiasm did change, what caused it to change?

It was important to have these questions answered because BTU had been experiencing the attrition of its African-American students. That is, during the matriculation of undergraduate African-American students from the fall of 1987 to the fall of 1992, a study showed that the university lost 25% to 33% of these students by the end of their second year (*Chancellor's Task Force on Student Retention*, 1997). Moreover, "in the two-year and six-year cohorts, 40% to 50% of African American students that drop out have GPAs above 2.0" (p.11). In addition, these questions became even more compelling because I had African-American friends who were in doctoral programs at other PWIs whose unhappy experiences were similar to those of Black undergraduate students at their universities.

I knew I would not be able to identify with these students as far as their undergraduate experiences at a PWI because I had attended a small private historically Black university in the Deep South. At this university, I was given a lot of support and encouragement. In addition, my professors knew me and I knew them. With their support and encouragement, I performed well and graduated with honors. In addition, they strongly encouraged me to continue my education; one professor took it upon herself to mail applications to my home.

Because I was a study skills instructor and my university experiences were different from these students, I wanted to know how best to help those who took the courses. Moreover, I wanted to view the struggles they talked about through their lens while attending BTU. Because of my concern and interest in the experiences of these Black students, I became determined to conduct this study.

My familiarity and teaching experiences with the Study Skills for College (SSC) courses, SSC 100 and 101, made my role as the researcher more resonant. My career with these courses spanned a period from 1995 to 1999. Specifically, as a discussion instructor for SSC 101, I had the opportunity to supervise a number of undergraduate teaching assistants (UTAs) whose jobs were to help students enrolled in the course apply various learning strategies. I also worked with the undergraduate teaching assistants in a hands-on mentoring course. Moreover, I designed another SSC course (SSC 200) as a future offering and had been a contributor to the many changes the courses had undergone through the years. Furthermore, I completed a small study that had focused on the perceptions of SSC 101 students from various ethnicities regarding their learning experiences at BTU (Johnson, 1998). The study concluded that students were motivated to learn when there were interactions with professors and when the course material was relevant to their experience. Findings also revealed that collaborative learning was pleasant (motivating) for some students but was not beneficial for other students. In addition, the study showed that students were motivated to excel in their other courses when they reflected on previous academic performances and used the information learned in the SSC course.

The perspective I brought to this study from my previous study was that both the academic and social environment determined whether these students excelled at the university. This brief glimpse into the perceptions of students from various ethnic backgrounds motivated me to focus specifically on the experiences of Black students who enrolled in Study Skills for College courses.

B. The Students

Eight Black students volunteered to participate in this study for the academic year of 1998/1999. There were four males and four females. Because one of the students identified himself as Caribbean American and not African American, the ethnic term "Black" was used in this study. All of the students had completed only one of the Study Skills for College (SSC 100 or SSC 101) courses at this PWPI. Six students took the summer seminar course, SSC 100, and two students took SSC 101. SSC 101 was not a required course.

However, students who participated in the Student Development Program (SDP) at BTU were required to take the summer seminar course, SSC 100.

Generally, although these students had enrolled in an SSC course, they considered themselves successful in high school. The parents of some of these students were also well educated. Moreover, they described their economic backgrounds as being middle class or working class. A profile of each student is discussed in the following section so that the reader can become familiar with these students.

1. Darnell

Darnell, a junior from New York City, identified himself as Caribbean American because his family immigrated from an island in the Caribbean when he was a preteen. He attended a large, predominantly Black high school in New York City. Darnell came to Big-Time University during the spring semester at the age of 16 because he skipped two grades in high school. He graduated with a 95 percent grade point average. He majored in computer engineering at BTU and hoped to obtain a master's in engineering management. The younger of two children, Darnell was the first to go to college in his family. He described his family's economic status as being middle class. He took the SSC 100 course the summer after his first semester at the university because in his words, "My dean told me I had to." He explained, "I got a B for sociology, a B for math, um a B or C for writing. I had an F for digital logic and some other course I took. I can't think of it now." He stated, "before I came to college, I don't think I've gotten like a C or D in anything. I never failed a course in my life."

2. Bryan

Bryan was a senior from Queens, New York and was an only child of a working class family. Neither of his parents attended college, and he was the first to go to college in his family. He attended a small predominantly Black high school and graduated with a B average. Bryan majored in information studies at Big-Time University. During his freshman year, his GPA went from a 2.8 to a 2.5. He took SSC 100 the summer after his freshman year.

3. Stacy

Stacy, the younger of two children, was a sophomore majoring in Speech Pathology and Psychology from southern New York. She described her family's economic status as being middle class. She attended a predominantly Black high school with a student population of about "two thousand" and graduated with a "B" or "B+" average. She planned to continue her education upon graduation from Big-Time University. Only one of Stacy's parents, her mother, was a college graduate who was also planning to pursue a master's degree in education. During her first semester at BTU, Stacy dropped two of the five classes she had. Even though her GPA was a 2.9, she said, "I could have done better considering I only had three classes." Stacy took SSC 101 the second semester of her freshman year on her advisor's recommendation. In her words, "I was just like o.k. Since ya'll are recommending it, it can't kill me." Because she performed well in the course, she was nominated and received an undergraduate teaching assistant (UTA) position with SSC 101. She held the position for one semester.

4. Imani

Imani, an only child, was a senior majoring in speech communication at BTU. She attended a predominantly Black high school located in an all Black county in Maryland. She described her family's economic status as being middle class. Both of her parents graduated from college. Imani attended a predominantly Black "magnet" high school. She took AP courses in high school but did not take the exams to get credits for college. Imani stated that the reason she did not take the tests was because "I just didn't feel like it." She graduated from high school with a 3.7 grade point average. She planned to attend law school. After her first semester at BTU, Imani said, "I got a 2.6, and here that's a B−. That wasn't satisfactory for me. I cried [because] I'm coming from [high] school making a 3.7. I saw that something had to be changed. And so my second semester, I really did more"; her GPA for that semester was a 3.2. Imani took SSC 101 the first semester of her sophomore year because, in her words, "somebody before told me that is was an easy class."

5. Larry

Larry, the oldest of three children, was from New York City and was a senior majoring in information management and technology. He planned to become a teacher. His mother attended a community college but did not finish. His father did not attend college. He described his family's economic status as being middle class. Larry graduated from a small, racially mixed high school in New York City. He graduated with a B or B+ grade point average. After his first semester at BTU, his GPA was a 2.7. He said, "I was disappointed with one of my grades. . . . I should have gotten a higher grade in that class." He maintained the same GPA the following semester. He took SSC 100 the summer after his freshman year and the summer before he entered his senior year.

6. *Kenya*

Kenya, the older of two children, was a junior majoring in child and family studies. She was from New York City and attended a large racially mixed high school. Kenya graduated high school with a C+ grade point average. She planned to obtain a master's in public administration and later open up a community center for inner city youths. She was the first to attend college in her working class family. During her freshman year as an engineering student at BTU, Kenya's GPA went from a 2.7 to a 1.9. "I know for a lot of people it's the opposite, [but] I really was not liking engineering, and I was having a hard time with the math." Therefore, she switched majors. She took SSC 100 the summer after her freshman year.

7. *Tina*

Tina, the youngest of three children, was from central New York. She was a sophomore majoring in public policy affairs. Only one of her parents, her mother, graduated from college. She described her family's status as middle class. Tina attended a racially mixed high school and graduated with a B+ average. She took AP courses in high school but did not take the exams to get credits for college. She explained that she did not take the tests because "I just doubted myself." She planned to go to law school. After her first semester at BTU, Tina's GPA was a 1.4. "I was so upset with myself," she said, "but I knew it wasn't because I wasn't a good student." Because of personal problems, Tina said she was not going to class often. However, even though her situation was better and her GPA rose a little the following semester, she was still on academic probation. She took SSC 100 the summer after her freshman year.

8. *Terrell*

Terrell, a junior from Brooklyn, New York, majored in information studies and technology. In a family he deemed as middle class, he was a middle child of five children, two of whom were adopted. Neither of his parents attended college. He graduated from a small, racially mixed high school with a B average. Terrell's GPA went from a 1.8 to a 2.4 his freshman year at BTU. He took SSC 100 the summer after his sophomore year.

2.7 THE HISTORY, CHARACTERISTICS AND PERCEIVED BENEFITS OF THE STUDY SKILLS COURSES AT BIG-TIME UNIVERSITY

The first study skills course was created in the early 1960s. It was a remedial noncredit course created to help underprepared students admitted into the university. These students were usually in the athletic program. The current professor and director, Dr. Brown, stated that the course was a "skills and drills" course that proved to be ineffective since the course enrollment decreased significantly over a period of years. She identified skills and drills as that of

> just practicing a particular skill. So, whether it's a decoding or a skill to teach students how to break down prefixes and suffixes and root words, it was really based on constant repetition.

She also added that the course

> was presented in such a way where everyone listened to a new lecture. In other words, it wasn't used on material they were actually studying in another class. Instead, someone would get up there and lecture for ten minutes and then you would take your notes. . . . Then you would get graded on the set of notes that you took.

Dr. Brown pointed out that when she began teaching the course in the early 1990s, the enrollment had decreased to ten students.

Since its creation, the course had undergone several changes. That is, it was moved from the School of Education to the College of Arts and Sciences. Later, it became a Nonarts and Science course (NAS 100) offered through the philosophy department. Unfortunately, due to the large number of Black students enrolled in the course, these students viewed the acronym, NAS, as meaning "Niggers Are Stupid" (Arno, 1987, p. 44). The study skills course also changed its content and purpose several times under different directors. In the next two sections, I discuss the revised version of the first study skills course and the creation of another SSC course at BTU.

2.8 STUDY SKILLS FOR COLLEGE 101: "THE LAST GAS STATION ON THE THRUWAY"

In 1991, under the direction of Dr. Brown, the first study skills course was restructured with the assistance of Dr. White, the Reading and Language Arts chairperson in the School of Education, and became known as Study Skills for College (SSC 101). Dr. White submitted the course for credit approval to the School of Education and then to the university senate. The course had to be presented before the university senate because it was moved from one school to another, the course name was changed, and there was no SSC department. The Study Skills for College (SSC 101) course would be based in the Reading and Language Arts Department and students elected to take this course. After the course became a credit bearing offering in the School of

Education, the enrollment increased significantly. There have been almost two thousand students who have taken the course since 1991.

SSC 101, which was taught during the fall and spring semesters, taught students particular strategies and asked them to use the strategies in their other courses. Some of the topics in this course focused on syllabus examination, course structure, time management, note taking, reading, procrastination, motivation, stress, and academic dishonesty. SSC 101 had several layers (lecture, recitation or discussion sections, and one-on-one conferences) that developed through the years. According to Dr. Brown, the purpose of SSC 101 was to

> build students' confidence in helping them to get control of their education. That is, I think it's my major reason for teaching the course. The other thing is really getting students to see how they learn and how to pick apart and unpack, if you will, a curriculum or syllabus so that students are not intimidated by the academic challenges in whatever course they're taking but have developed the skills to meet the challenge.

She further added,

> Obviously, we try to teach the students to transfer [the study] skills now from one course to another. My hope would be that they would be able to transfer [those skills] throughout their college career and when they're working [on their jobs] or in their personal lives.

Discussion instructors, who were graduate students, were added later because of the growing enrollment. They taught the discussion or recitation sections and supervised the undergraduate teaching assistants. The vice chancellor's office at BTU provided the funds to pay the discussion instructors.

Because there was no SSC course next in the sequence and some students wanted to remain involved with the course, Dr. Brown created the undergraduate teaching assistant (UTA) position. Students holding this position had taken the SSC 101 course and had performed exceptionally well. At one-on-one weekly conferences, they taught students enrolled in the course how to apply the strategies to their other courses. In addition, students enrolled in SSC 101 received points toward their grade for attending the mandatory UTA conferences. Moreover, it was mandatory that UTAs attend every lecture and a hands-on mentoring course. In the hands-on mentoring course, the UTAs role-played and discussed the strategies and problems they were having with the students. Dr. Brown and SSC discussion instructors taught the hands-on mentoring course. The UTAs also met each week with a discussion instructor to discuss their assigned students' progress and other issues. Those UTAs, who were in their second semester of tutoring, were paid from funds provided by the vice chancellor's office. The professor, discussion instructor, and other undergraduate teaching assistants nominated future undergraduate teaching assistants. According to Dr. Brown, adding this feature to the course was effective at two levels:

> Its very effective for the UTA because it is, in fact, the opportunity for the UTA to use the skills once again and to sit through the course once again and benefit from that experience because change does not occur quickly. And some students need a second semester of exposure to really understand that. So that's the first level. Second thing I think that there are a lot of students who [need] somebody that they can talk about course work with and feel comfortable and then share other issues that are problematic at a peer level.

Unfortunately, there were not many Black undergraduate teaching assistants for SSC 101. Dr. Brown stressed that "it's a real frustration with me because it's decreased every year for me . . . the minority enrollment in my [SSC 101] classes is decreasing every year." Furthermore, she did not know why this was happening. Nevertheless, according to Dr. Brown, there had been a quarter to a third of Black students who served as UTAs. She pointed out that "I can only nurture the kids that I do get. And they are the kids that I will look to see, you know, if the student's somebody that I could really get to be a UTA and be more visible in the program."

Students had also used an SSC 101 textbook. SSC 101 students chose to do several assignments from the textbook. The assignments consisted of exam experiments, paper experiments, open experiments, faculty and student interviews, peer observations, and a group project (Blumin, 1997). In addition, students turned in weekly journal entries and took quizzes. Students met with their discussion instructors to set up due dates for the assignments.

The exam experiment was one assignment that helped SSC 101 students to prepare and organize information to study for an exam in another course. The goal of the exam experiment was to prevent students from cramming the night before a test. Therefore, they created a study schedule, outlines, concept maps, and possible test questions to prepare for the exam. Another assignment was the paper experiment. It enabled students to organize information to write a paper for one of their courses in a given number of days, prior to the paper's due date. The students created a writing schedule, outline, and concept maps to write their papers. The goal of the paper experiment was to prevent students from writing a paper the night before it was due. The open experiment gave students the opportunity to solve personal or academic problems. That is, students chose to solve problems that pertained to procrastination, motivation, time management, roommate problems, managing money, and choosing a major. They identified the problem and devised strategies and a plan to possibly solve the situation. Later, they graphically illustrated the positive and negative aspects of trying their strategies. They also wrote a reflection about the experience.

Faculty interviews offered students a chance to discuss with three of their professors the expectations for the course and other academic issues. They were encouraged by Dr. Brown, discussion instructors, and UTAs to interview professors for their most difficult courses. Students prepared questions in advance, and they interviewed their professors during office hours. Next, the students wrote a summary of the interviews and presented their findings to their classmates during recitation. For the student interviews, SSC 101 students had the opportunity to choose five students from one of their current courses to obtain strategies and perspectives of that course. They also had the option to interview students who had previously taken that particular course with the same professor. The steps for this assignment were the same as those for the faculty interviews.

Students who chose to do the peer observation assignment worked together to help each other solve a personal or academic problem. This assignment only involved two students, and they were usually from the same recitation or discussion section. The problems were usually the same as those mentioned earlier with the open experiment. The two students gave each other strategies to solve a problem and then each initiated the suggested strategies. Later, they wrote a reflection about this experience.

The group project came at the end of the semester. Its purpose was to encourage collaborative learning. SSC 101 students collaborated as a group as they created and used strategies they had learned in the course to solve hypothetic academic and personal situations. Students presented these situations through skits, commercials, talk shows, game shows, and videos. The situations usually pertained to issues mentioned earlier with the open experiment and the peer observation assignment. However, they had presented topics that concerned drinking and drug use. Moreover, the students graded each other's projects. Nevertheless, if the group projects were not done correctly, the discussion instructor intervened and did the grading.

It was mandatory for students to turn in journal assignments every week. Students chose to write a personal journal or an academic journal. Personal journals gave students the opportunity to write about events and situations that were currently occurring in their lives. Some of the topics that students wrote about were courses, professors, roommates, pledging a fraternity or sorority, promiscuity, AIDS, and sexual orientations. With the academic journals, students reflected on a particular strategy such as note taking or reading that they had used. The discussion instructors read these journals and made comments. Commenting on the students' journal topics had always been beneficial for me because I not only had seen how the students applied the strategies or how they were dealing with personal challenges, but also I had gotten to know the students as individuals. Attendance and participation were highly stressed for this course. If students did not attend lecture, discussion or recitation, and UTA conferences, they lost points toward their grade.

Even though honor students enrolled in this course, those students who had learning disabilities, those students who had barely been accepted into the university, those students who were on academic probation, and those students who wanted to do better to get into more competitive university programs also enrolled. Some "are just students who want a good grade and, therefore, think SSC is an easy A," according to Dr. Brown. For those students who were on probation, Dr. Brown stated that SSC 101 was "the last gas station on the thruway." SSC 101 usually received these range of students during the fall semesters. However, it was during the spring semesters that the course had an influx of students who were in academic jeopardy. Their academic advisors usually suggested that they take this course. Only freshmen, sophomores, and juniors were allowed to take the course. However, seniors were admitted into the course via a waiver obtained from Dr. Brown.

Dr. Brown believed that students not only gained a positive attitude from completing the course, but they also

> take away an image that not all professors and instructors are the most horrible people in the world. I also think they take away a feeling that if they are in trouble in another class, they know there are people to go to rather than walking away from the challenge in that other class.

2.9 STUDY SKILLS FOR COLLEGE 100: THE SUMMER SEMINAR

Study Skills for College 100 (SSC 100), which was also based in the Reading and Language Arts Department, was a credit bearing summer seminar course created for the Student Development Program (SDP) in 1992. The Student Development Program provided students who were not meeting the academic demands of the university with a comprehensive learning experience to increase their skills and confidence (Division of Student Support and Retention, 1999). Students who participated in this program were required to take SSC 100. Nonetheless, although the summer seminar course is no longer a requirement for this program, the students in this study had completed the course before this decision. The topics that were discussed in SSC 100 pertained to syllabus examination, course structure, professors, course material, procrastination, motivation, time management, and so on. The goal of the course was "to help students explore their own issues." Second semester freshmen, sophomores, juniors, and students entering their senior year took this course. However, a large number of these students who had enrolled in this summer course were Black. Graduate students who were instructors for SSC 101 taught the course. Since 1992, almost six hundred students had taken this course.

The summer course work consisted of three "what if" assignments, three in-class essays, a group project, and a final reflective essay. Attendance and participation counted highly, and students lost points toward their grade for not attending class. There was no textbook for this course. For the "what if" assignments, each student presented an academic or social problem he or she was encountering to other students in the class. The students collaborated to help each other solve the problem by suggesting strategies. After applying these suggested strategies, each student was required to report the results to the other students in class. With the in-class essays, the students answered the following questions consecutively: (1) what characteristics do you look for in the professors that teach your courses and how do you use that information; (2) what information do you use to know how to accomplish learning the material in your courses; and (3) when you initially attend a course, what do you observe about the course that confirms to you that you made the right decision by registering for it?

The process for the group project was the same as that of SSC 101. However, it was the instructor who did the grading and not the students. The final assignment for SSC 100 was the reflective essay. Students were asked to not only reread their in-class essays, but they also wrote about the changes they had experienced during the six weeks. They were also asked to discuss how these changes might impact them in the fall semester. According to Dr. Brown, the end results of this course were that students not only took away discipline but also "a willingness to have explored their role in their learning."

In Chapter Three, the high school experiences of the Black students in this study are presented. In addition, I discuss the academic and social difficulties the students experienced prior to taking SSC as they tried to separate from past academic communities and transition into a predominantly White environment. I also report the learning strategies the students used.

Chapter Three

Between Two Worlds: Making the Transition

Moving from a high school environment into a university setting would be challenging for all students, but for the Black students in this study, the move had been very difficult. Tinto (1993) described this move as the separation stage because it required students to disassociate themselves from past communities. Once in the university, students were supposed to experience the transition stage. This was just before they fully adopted the norms and behavioral patterns of the new environment and after separating from the old ones (Tinto, 1993). Because of alienation, racism, and other academic issues in their freshman year, the students were never able to make a complete transition into BTU and did not experience Tinto's incorporation or integration stage.

In this alienating academic and social atmosphere, the learning strategies they used prior to taking the SSC course were adopted out of a desperate attempt to survive or "get by" and were often unsuccessful. In the next section, I present these students' high school experiences. This section is followed by the social and academic challenges the students encountered at BTU and the strategies they used to learn course material.

3.1 THEIR HIGH SCHOOL YEARS

Before matriculating into BTU, seven of the eight students in this study attended high schools where they were the racial majority. Four attended primarily Black high schools while the other four attended racially mixed high schools. Only one of the eight students attended a high school where he was a racial minority. As shown in Chapter Two, the students were generally successful in high school. Their grade point averages ranged from C+ to A, with most of the students falling on the high end of the spectrum.

Those students who attended predominantly Black high schools described them as being supportive environments. For example, Stacy, who attended a large predominantly Black high school, said that the staff (Black and White) "were really caring and concerned for the students' well-being." Moreover, she pointed out,

> My teachers and advisors were very concerned about my grades and future. When I had problems, or they saw that something wasn't right, they were very supportive and helpful. They were individuals that I could talk to.

She gave an example to illustrate how concerned one of her White teachers was when she was not performing well in his course. She stated,

> I remember my twelfth grade English teacher had noticed that I had been skipping his class lately and not doing my assignments. He quickly pulled me aside and told me that this wasn't like me and that he was concerned. It was nothing big. I just had a typical case of senioritis.

Because Stacy "knew the teachers" and they "knew your name," she had no problems approaching them because "it was more personal." In addition, she liked the way one of her African-American teachers got students involved in the lesson, even if they did not read the assignments. To get the students involved, he would say, "Like Stacy just explained this, what do you think of that?" According to Stacy, his technique "made you participate" without embarrassment.

Like Stacy, Bryan, who attended a small predominantly Black high school, believed that his teachers were supportive. He described his teachers as having "more time" for students because "basically you walk in [to their classrooms] and they're there." He found this comforting since his high school had the reputation of accepting students who "got kicked out of other schools." In addition, he stated that "if you look like you had a chance to go to college, [the teachers] were very supportive. If I didn't have money to fill out an application, [the school] would give me a waiver. Like I didn't pay for college applications or SAT tests or anything like that."

For those who attended racially mixed high schools where they were the racial majority, the environment was still supportive and nurturing. For example, Kenya said there were two African-American teachers who had "such high expectations for us." She continued,

> They were very hard on us, but at the same time, they were very nurturing. And if someone was doing badly in class, and they knew that, because they looked

at every student as having potential, especially like the kids who would get into trouble, they specifically took them to the side and talked with them.

Tina, who also attended a racially mixed high school, emphasized that "all my teachers knew me. They knew I was a jokester and stuff like that." They also "stayed on my back and made sure I did what I had to do to get out." For example, in her AP social studies class, she said the class was very hard and the White teacher (who called her by the nickname "T. W.") did not let her get away with turning assignments in late. She appreciated that because "his expectations made me want to do better."

As for Larry, who attended a "student-centered," "alternative school," he appreciated the "open classes" and being on a "first name basis with teachers." Moreover, he stated that his racially mixed high school "was kind of set up like [how] recitation is set up here (BTU). We didn't sit up in desks in rows and things like that." In addition, he pointed out that there were "not a lot of tests." Instead, students wrote papers in subjects like math and science. He liked this style of learning because "you're explaining yourself." He continued, "A lot of people know a lot of things but to be able to explain it and be able to take somebody through it, that's when the understanding comes into play."

Terrell was the only student who attended a high school where he was the racial minority. Even though the high school was in an Italian neighborhood, Hispanics made up the racial majority. "It was a more balanced ratio my freshman year in high school, and then as my dean would put it, he went through the cleansing phase." Terrell said, "they (school) didn't want what they termed as ghetto people in the school . . . They kept (a) [those] on the sports teams or (b) what they would call me, an Uncle Tom." Nevertheless, he stated, "Whenever I use to mess up, [the teachers] would get on me."

Three students who attended inner city high schools did not believe that the schools prepared them for college. For example, Darnell, who attended a predominantly Black high school said, "My high school did not challenge me enough. I didn't need to study to complete course work at any time during high school. Thus, I came to college with that mentality." Sadly, he pointed out, "I never had consequences for not putting in those extra hours." Even though Bryan had supportive teachers, he said, "We were behind everybody else. While everybody else was reading books like *Othello* and things like that, we were like, 'what's that?' We weren't reading like Shakespeare and things like that until my senior year." Bryan's and Darnell's statements support the findings of Richardson, Simmons, and Santos (1987) who concluded that minority students attending inner city high schools often were not placed in competitive environments, and they lacked the course offerings needed to succeed in a four-year college program.

For some of these students, however, the high school learning environments were perceived as nurturing, supportive and encouraging. Even though some felt that they were not completely prepared for college, all of the students had performed well in high school. However, as they tried to make the separation from their old learning communities and attempted to transition into a new academic milieu, they experienced difficulties and challenges.

3.2 GUESTS AT AN IVORY TOWER: IT'S A DIFFERENT WORLD AT BTU

Unlike White students who enter a predominantly White academic environment, Black students are challenged to make adjustments as "guests in someone else's house" (Turner, 1994, p. 355). According to Turner (1994), students of color are "guests [who] have no history in the house they occupy. There are no photographs on the wall that reflect their image. Their paraphernalia, paintings, scents, and sounds do not appear in the house" (p. 356). Therefore, these students have to contend with the stress of transitioning into the mainstream university while trying to separate from past learning communities where they have been comfortable.

Moving from a predominantly Black learning environment into a predominantly White environment caused Bryan not to like BTU. He stated that, because he did not like the university when he arrived the fall semester of his freshman year, he wanted to return home. He said BTU "wasn't high school. It was new people and things like that." Furthermore, "the people weren't really what I expected. I guess I wasn't what they expected either." Therefore, he felt that the university was not "welcoming." In addition, despite the fact that he was not an athlete, people often perceived him as such. This stereotype became a reality while registering for classes his first semester. Bryan, who is six feet four, explained

> I was going to register for classes, . . . and I couldn't get into this one class. So, I had to get a waiver and I went to go see [this woman in the registrar's office]. When I went to go see her, she just looked at me and she was like 'O.k. here's the waiver.' I took the waiver and went back to give it to [the people at the registration booth]. They looked at it, and they were like 'Something is wrong with it' [and] that I have to go back to [the woman in the registrar's office]. So, I went back to her and I said, 'They said something is wrong with this, and I need to um do something with it to get into the class.' She looked at me and she was like um 'Well, why didn't your coach,' she said something about a coach. I was like 'What do you mean? I don't play a sport.' She was like 'You don't play a sport?' I was like 'Nah.' She was like, 'If I had known that, you wouldn't have even got-

ten into the class.' I was like 'Oh.' She said, 'Since I gave you the waiver all ready then take it.'

It appeared to Bryan that a Black male who was over six feet tall at a predominantly White university was perceived by White students and staff as only attending for one reason—to play a sport.

Like Bryan, Stacy commented that she "hated the university when [she] first got here":

I remember calling one of my friends [back home] and crying over her voicemail [because] I didn't have any friends [here] and there was no one to talk to. The only person I knew was nowhere to be found, but that was the first few days. The day I finally found the [Black] girl I knew, we met up with this [other Black] girl on my floor who had just moved in. Everything after that was cool. We're all really close friends. It was hard to meet a lot of Black people on campus if you didn't live in CC (Cooper and Crawford dorm). Since we were in Simpson [Hall], an upper class mostly white dorm, we were basically by ourselves.

Similarly, Imani lived in an "all white dorm, an all white Jewish dorm" and felt that Blacks were distributed thinly throughout campus. She viewed the dormitory situation as being "really ridiculous." Her situation was awkward because "me and my Black friend, that lived next door to me, were the only Black people on our floor. We could not believe that. It seemed that all the Black people lived in [the] Cooper and Crawford [dormitory]." However, she pointed out that the university had deviated from placing a majority of the Black students in the Cooper and Crawford dormitory.

Unlike the other students who entered BTU in the fall, Darnell came to BTU during the spring semester at the age of 16. He said, "I felt very alone because I didn't know anyone and I was in a strange place." Darnell was matriculating from a predominantly Black high school. Nevertheless, he "loved the environment." He pointed out that "people were very friendly and usually said 'hi' to you as they passed. That was comforting, but I felt very alone."

These findings support D'Augelli and Hashberger's (1993) conclusion that when Black students arrived on predominantly White campuses, they knew fewer students than their White counterparts and came from high schools and communities where they were the majority. Bryan, Stacy, Imani and Darnell, who came from predominantly Black high schools, felt as though they were now "distinct minorities" on BTU's campus (p. 68). These Black students had become "lost in a sea of white faces" (Feagin, Vera, & Imani, 1996, p. 39) and did not feel at home. In addition, they were not entering into an academic milieu where there were a large number of professors and administrators who were Black (Bello-Ogunu, 1997). As Ron Wakabayashi pointed out in Turner (1994), minority students often feel unable to "relax and put [their] feet up on the table" (p. 357) in predominantly White institutions.

While some students in this study arrived on campus the fall and spring semesters, there were some students who came during the summer before their freshman year. They participated in BTU's six-week, Pre-College Summer Program. Despite their participation in the program, the separation stage for those students was still difficult. Terrell, who had been mistaken by students and university staff as a BTU football player, said that he cried the first day he arrived at the university because "that was the first time I had ever been away from home. That was the first time Dad was a long distance phone call away." In addition, he stated that "there was no family here and everyone was looking out for his or her own. It was a tough first week." Although a large number of Black students participated in this program, perhaps the idea of not knowing anyone took a toll on Terrell. This particular situation reaffirms D'Augelli and Hashberger's (1993) study that Black students come to predominantly White campuses knowing few students.

Unlike Terrell, Larry, who was also perceived as a BTU football player, had friends attending the university, so he "was already introduced to the whole social aspect of [the university]." However, Larry's major concern pertained to academics. He stressed,

> The only agitation was just that I didn't know what to expect academically speaking you know. . . . So, I mean in a lot of ways just from the history and tradition and what [BTU] is known for, it painted like a threatening picture in terms of like, I thought I was going to come here and be surrounded by I guess quote unquote geeks or nerds or whatever you want to call it. I mean just individuals that are exceptionally smart, geniuses per say.

Larry also shared that he knew that taking tests would be a challenge for him because he did not "take a lot of tests in high school. So learning how to take tests would be a little bit difficult in comparison to other students." Previously, it was pointed out that Larry wrote papers instead of taking tests in subjects like math and science at his high school. Therefore, coming into a new academic environment where there would be tests caused the separation stage to be much more challenging for him.

According to Tinto (1993), separating from past communities is particularly difficult for minority students, because "separation may represent a major shift in the way they construct their lives" (p. 97). For these Black students, their lives changed dramatically when they entered BTU. That is, they left a familiar and comfortable inclusive environment and matriculated into an alienating milieu with primarily White students and faculty who sometimes held stereotypical beliefs. In short, they entered into this ivory tower as "guests" rather than members who could relax and put their feet up on the table like White students.

3.3 BEING BLACK IN THE CLASSROOM: "I JUST FELT OUT OF THE LOOP"

For this group of Black students, separating from past learning environments and transitioning into the university classroom was another challenge. This challenge usually began on the first day of the fall semester of their freshman year when these students walked into the classroom. For example, Kenya, who was accustomed to smaller high school classes, stated that she "just felt out of the loop" while sitting in a lecture that contained four hundred students. She felt this way because "it was just like [the professor] was just talking to the masses you know. He wasn't talking to me." Furthermore, she maintained that "there was no interaction" among the students and the professor. Bryan concurred with Kenya by stating:

> I couldn't believe how many people were actually in there because my high school is real small. And for me to sit in like a big like auditorium with one guy sitting up there speaking and like a hundred kids sitting in one place just taking notes or whatever, it was kind of boring.

It was obvious why these students felt out of the loop in these large lectures. That is, they were no longer individuals as they were in their small high school classes. They felt like "numbers" in a sea of white faces where very few students were of their race. In addition, if these students were the only Blacks in the lecture, the experience of alienation became more profound. For instance, Imani, who grew up in an all Black county, struck at the heart of the matter by emphasizing that she "felt intimidated in classes sometimes. . . . [because] when I was in class, I was the only black person there. I was like 'Whoa this can't be when I was coming from a high school where there was nothing but Black people.'" Apparently, Imani was experiencing the disjuncture between her all Black learning environment and that of a predominantly White learning environment. There was no sense of solidarity or comfort for her. In support of Bello-Ogunu (1997), he pointed out that many Black students begin and complete their academic careers as the only Black in some courses.

For some students, being the only Black in the classroom caused them to be cautious when voicing an opinion on some topics. For example, Kenya stated,

I felt more cautious of the things that I said once I realized [I was the only Black person]. [I didn't want to] offend anyone and [wanted to make sure] that no one would feel uncomfortable and that the climate of the classroom would be o.k.

Kenya also made it clear that she did not want to throw around the "race card" on many issues because she did not want to be viewed as a troublemaker.

While Kenya tried to be more cautious when voicing her opinion, Terrell was more daring by presenting his world view in his assignments. For example, when he had to write a fairy tale about a friend for his writing class, he "connected it to real life situations." He embellished the story of Cinderella with details from his own experience as a former resident of Brooklyn, New York. He stated, "Like instead of the coach, [Cinderella] takes the train. Uh instead of a ball, she went to a dance. Like instead of like mice, they were roaches." His character returned to the projects after the dance. Unfortunately, his White writing teacher was angry at his creative style and was unable to understand why the ghetto did not turn into a condominium. Terrell pointed out to her that there was no such thing as a fairy tale for his character; "It was time reality hit." He received an "A" on his paper, but not without being confronted for breaking the rules of the teacher's assignment or agenda. Terrell's situation supported Goldblatt's (1995) argument that

to ask students from marginalized communities to take on academic discourse as their own is to invite them into a world where they have no power, requiring that they check their former badges of power at the door (p. 26–27).

However, in Terrell's case, he refused to follow the rules or check his former badge of power at the door.

Ideally, the college classroom should be a free communicative environment where students express their opinions and feel a sense of belonging. However, these students felt the stress of being a "distinct minority" (D'Augelli & Hashberger, 1993, p.68) in the classroom. These academic and social stressors made them grow more distant from the predominantly White learning community. Therefore, it appeared that they were still in the separation stage and had not begun to transition into the classroom environment at BTU.

3.4 "I FIGURED [THE PROFESSOR] WOULDN'T BE ABLE TO HELP ME OUTSIDE OF CLASS"

Going to a professor for assistance was not easy for these students the first semester of their freshman year. For example, Stacy, who was having problems in statistics, said that she "didn't understand what [the professor] was talking about in class, so [she] figured [the professor] wouldn't be able to help [her] outside of class." Instead, she studied with another Black student. Unfortunately, this technique did not work because she received a "D" on the first test and an "F" on the second one. Thus, she dropped the course.

Stacy also dropped her writing course because she had become ill and was behind in her work. Rather than approach the professor and discuss her situation, she sent an e-mail. I asked Stacy why she did not discuss the situation with the professor in person. She remarked that approaching the professor was not as personal as it was in high school. In high school, "[she] knew the teachers [and; therefore,] it was more personal."

As for Bryan who was having difficulties in philosophy, he went to the teaching assistant. However, the visit did not help because Bryan "just didn't understand [the material] at all." As a result, he flunked the first test. He thought about dropping the class but decided to stay. Nevertheless, he did pass the course with a "C."

By the second semester, some students did feel more comfortable approaching their professors. For example, Imani said her math professor "was really into helping people out in understanding [the material]." He gave review sheets, and they met often during his office hours to go over math problems. As a result, she did very well and received a B+ in the course. Knowing that she did not perform well in math the first semester with another professor, I asked why she did not go to him for help. She remarked, "My teacher didn't seem too enthusiastic, so I was like he's not so why should I." He also was not as open and did not give review sheets.

Obviously, students like Stacy had not forgotten the support and nurturing they received from their high school teachers. Therefore, instead of going to the professors, they went to the teaching assistant or another student. Perhaps, they felt more comfortable with the teaching assistants and peers because, unlike professors, they were not intimidating. However, when professors were open and appeared helpful, students like Imani were more apt to seek help. Because these students were in the separation stage and had not fully begun to transition into this alienating environment, they were less likely to approach the professor when they had problems. Along with the social pressures these students had to confront in their freshmen year, in the next sections, I discuss the strategies they used to cope with the demands of their course work.

3.5 "TO READ OR NOT TO READ": READING STRATEGIES USED PRIOR TO TAKING SSC

As indicated earlier, these Black students were separating from inclusive high school communities and entering into an alienating environment in their freshmen year. Therefore, learning the course material and succeeding in this predominantly White environment made the experience much more challenging. In this emotionally charged "sink-or-swim" situation, students often used learning strategies that were haphazard and sometimes counterproductive. Typically, for example, students relied upon obtaining the information from lecture rather than the assigned reading. As Tina pointed out,

> The majority of the time, I didn't read [the book for my child development class], but when it came down to quizzes, I always got A's. I always knew what they were talking about in class [because] that class was basic common sense.

According to Tina, [the professor] "showed us clippings [and] different movies associated with the topics that we were dealing with." Therefore, "there was no need for just study study study." As a result, "you could get by without reading [because] the test came from the lectures and only two things usually came from the textbook." Because the course was "basic common sense" to Tina, she performed well on her quizzes without reading. However, because of personal problems, she did not attend this class often and, as a result, she received an "F" in the course.

Unlike Tina, Kenya stopped reading for one of her classes when she found the reading material too difficult. Therefore, she relied on the class discussions to get her through the course. For her sociology class, she explained,

> I just didn't read for the class. . . .It was very confusing to me because a lot of the arguments that were made were abstract and I didn't know how to deal with that at that time. . . .I didn't know what the teacher wanted—where he was headed. I'm going to be honest with you. I didn't   even study for that exam, but I passed just by reviewing my notes and the conversations we had in class. That was it.

She received a "C" on her first sociology test. She vaguely remembered what she made on her other two tests, but she said that she passed. I gathered from this comment and her facial expressions that the grades were not superior. Moreover, I observed that she was somewhat ashamed or reluctant to share those two grades.

While Kenya and Tina relied on the lectures to get their information, Bryan resorted to reading the assigned material with a friend. He explained,

> I be reading my [philosophy] book and he be reading his [philosophy] book. I mean we're just sitting there together and reading our books. Basically, we're studying the information by ourselves. . . . We talked about it after we finished.

This was not a good strategy because they still were not able to make sense out of the material when they discussed it. Bryan also pointed out that the readings were unusual because they were trying to "figure out the relationship between A or B or whatever." In addition, several times while they were reading, he said they would burst into laughter. Perhaps they found the material so outrageous, stressful and nerve wrecking until all they could do was laugh it off. In short, he said that this was his "worst" class because he " just could not get it," even when he sought help from the teaching assistant.

There were times when students read assigned reading materials only for specific reasons. For example, Stacy explained how she read in preparation for psychology quizzes and examinations:

> Before a quiz, [the teaching assistant] told us what we needed to know for the quiz [in] psychology. That's when I read and when I read that, I read it until I understood it. . . . Also um with the exam, [the professor] gave us the stuff on the web. He outlined the stuff you needed to know and that's what I read too.

As for her Biology class, she read only what was necessary to complete her Bio-creativity extra credit assignment. She said, "I used the textbook during [the making of] my flip book because I had to know about mitosis. So, I made a flip book of a cell joining with an egg and doing mitosis or miosis or whichever one it was." She also pointed out that she was angry that she bought the textbook since she had very little use for it. However, Stacy was not alone in her reasoning. Terrell and Darnell had the same beliefs as she. That is, when Terrell had to do a group project on drugs, he said, "We (group members) read to help us with the project. That's when we read." Darnell, who had to read to write a paper for his writing class, stated

> I read very little for [the paper]. But um I read enough where I could cite information out the books so I could support my argument but nothing more than that. I wrote a very good 10-page paper, and I'm proud of it.

Stacy, Terrell, and Darnell read what they had to in order to complete course work and nothing more.

Although most students read selectively just to do well on quizzes and papers, there were times when students read deeply and willingly. This often occurred when the readings were relevant and connected to real life experiences. For example, students who took courses in African-American Studies did not complain about the reading. In fact, they found pleasure in reading the books. For instance, Kenya said that reading books in her African-American Studies class was like "therapy" for her. In her words,

> They were books that I enjoyed so it was o.k. You know it was like pertaining to my life. You know things that I could relate to . . . things that I went through like

especially with *The Bluest Eye* (Morrison, 1972) and the identity crisis. So I read
a lot and there were things I was very passionate about, so that inspired me.

In addition, when it came time for a test, Kenya saw no need to study the
novel because she remembered the information in the book so well that she
"knew what was said on what page, what section, what position of the page it
was on, whether it was on the right or left." Because she saw herself in the book,
she felt a reason to read. In contrast, Kenya had avoided reading for her sociology class earlier, obtaining her information primarily from the lecture. She was
not able to connect her personal experiences to the information in the sociology
book as she had when she read the Toni Morrison novel. Larry, on the other
hand, was inspired to read in his health and exercise class. He found the reading
interesting because he wanted to "pick up on some ideas" about power lifting at
the time. Therefore, because Kenya and Larry had such personal connections
with the reading, they read deeply and purposefully.

Perhaps these students were in a culture shock or crisis when they used
these strategies because they were trying to survive academically in a strange
environment. Therefore, they resorted to using only the minimal reading
strategies they perceived would help them in their courses. Nevertheless, they
did read in a rich and purposeful way when the assigned readings were relevant to them. Thus, they were trying to make the transition into BTU.

3.6 "WHAT WAS ON THE OLD EXAMS, THAT'S WHAT I STUDIED"

Another strategy students used in their freshmen year was that of relying on
old examinations to study in some of their courses. These old examinations
were placed on reserve by some professors at BTU's main library. Imani, for
example, used old chemistry tests to prepare for each examination in the
course. She emphasized, "I just looked at the answers and tried to memorize
the questions and the answers that go along with it because [the professor]
didn't change his test very much." Unfortunately, her strategy was not a very
good one because she received a "D" on the test. Moreover, Imani's performance on the examinations did not encourage her to seek assistance from
the professor because she "really hated [the course and] wasn't that motivated
to do better."

While Imani did not succeed by using old tests, Stacy did. For her Biology
test, Stacy used a more focused strategy than Imani had. Stacy explained,

O.K. This is what I did. I took [the] old exams. The questions I got right on the
topic I got right, I didn't bother studying them because I knew I knew them. But

the stuff that I didn't get right, that's what I would study. . . . So, I would basically go over the questions I got wrong.

Thus, while Imani memorized the answers to her test, Stacy analyzed the test to see which questions she did not know well. In order to clarify the questions she got wrong, she went back to her lab book or textbook for the correct answer. As a result of this strategy, she performed well on her tests and earned a "B" for the class. Luckily for Stacy, her professor did not change his old examinations much. Unfortunately, Imani, who had been less strategic in her study habits, earned a "C+" in chemistry. She said, "my labs are what saved me because I got A's in my labs."

Even though Imani did not perform well on her tests, Stacy, who used strategic test-taking techniques, did. However, although Stacy did well on tests, she, as well as Imani, remained in an environment that alienated them.

3.7 NOTE TAKING: I WROTE "WHATEVER [THE PROFESSOR] WROTE ON THE BOARD"

Since they were not doing much reading their freshman year, the students were depending on the lectures to get their information. For example, Larry said that, because his psychology professor used overheads, he was able to get a lot of his information that way. In addition, because his professor elaborated on the topics, he "wrote down little stuff that came [in]to [his] head like things to help [him] remember it." In other words, by associating the topics learned with similar personal experiences, Larry was analyzing the information as he paraphrased it. As for Imani, who stated that she was not a good note taker, she wrote "key words" and went back to the book for clarification after lecture.

While Larry and Imani were active note-takers, Terrell only wrote "whatever [the professor] wrote on the board" for one of his classes. Apparently, Terrell was not making additional notations that could help him understand the lesson. Unfortunately, he mentioned that there were some classes in which he did not take any notes.

Sadly, students like Terrell appeared to have exhibited relatively passive behaviors while taking notes, only copying notes from the board. By not connecting the lecture notes to the book or personal experiences, their note-taking strategy became more literal than analytic.

In sum, Tinto's (1993) theory of student departure illustrated the typical pattern of integration into the academic and social environment of an institution through three stages: separation, transition, and incorporation. The separation stage required students to disassociate themselves from past communities (Tinto, 1993). For these Black students, the separation stage was very challenging because it was difficult to disconnect from inclusive learning communities where they felt comfortable and where most of them were in the racial majority. In addition, it was impossible for them to leave their Blackness or culture at the door of the ivory tower.

In general, they were not able to adopt the "new norms and patterns of behavior" (Tinto, 1993, p. 97) at BTU because of the alienation, subtle racism, and other academic issues they encountered outside and inside the classroom. Perhaps they used rudimentary strategies for reading, test-taking, and note-taking that were focused on "getting by" and surviving because they were not able to fully transition and integrate into the predominantly White academic mainstream. Study skills courses like the one the students eventually enrolled in were meant to ameliorate such problems. Therefore, in the next chapter, I discuss the strategies taught in the SSC courses in more detail, how the students fared beyond their freshman year, and the strategies they reported using.

Chapter Four

Study Skills for College Courses: Are they Assisting in the Transition?

While attempting to transition into BTU, students took the "Study Skills for College" (SSC) courses. Tinto (1987) argued that universities should help students make the transition into the academic and social environment by providing transition assistance programs. These programs focused on study skills, study habits, writing term papers, using the library, and social adjustments (Tinto, 1987).

Unfortunately at BTU, the stress to survive in an alienating environment probably made it difficult for the Black students in this study to use the SSC strategies. Instead, they continued to use strategies that were haphazard or geared toward "getting by." For example, both before and after taking the course, they read only the teacher's class notes, old examinations that some professors did not change, or material directly relevant to their lives. The conversations reported in this chapter showed that only three students used the strategies from the SSC courses, and these strategies did not always work. As illustrated in the previous chapter, these Black students had made neither a complete academic nor social transition into this university by the end of their freshman year. Ostensibly, courses like SSC should have helped them make the social and academic transition. However, as this chapter demonstrated, despite the wealth of strategies taught, students still failed to make a complete academic and social transition at BTU.

In the next section, I discuss the academic and social strategies taught in the SSC courses. This section is followed by the academic and social challenges these students continued experiencing after taking the SSC courses.

4.1 THE SSC STRATEGIES

The goals of the SSC courses were both academic and social. Academically, students were taught a variety of learning strategies that would assist them in their courses. Socially, students were encouraged to speak with their professors and to work with their peers. The strategies taught in SSC courses were premised on some assumptions about the university. That is, SSC teachers assumed that professors would expect students to read critically and strategically for an understanding or insight in their college classes. Next, it was assumed that professors would expect students to make connections between their textbooks and other concepts learned in class. Thus, the students would need to take detailed class notes when appropriate. In addition, it was assumed that professors would create new evaluation tools or tests rather than relying only on previous test items available to some students. Finally, it was assumed that students would seek out help from professors and peers without any difficulty. Based upon these assumptions, SSC teachers taught students various reading, test-taking, and note-taking strategies, as well as some social strategies such as collaborating with peers and seeking help from professors.

To begin, the students were taught a number of reading strategies including "SQ3R," "KWL," "PM2R," "SPARCS," and "MURDER" (Blumin, 1994; Blumin, 1997). Each letter in the acronym or word represented a step the students initiated while reading. For example, the steps for SQ3R required the students to *survey* the chapter by reading the headings and subheadings before engaging in the reading. Next, the students turned the headings and subheadings into *questions* and *read* for the answers. Without looking at the book, the students *recited* the answers to their questions. Finally, the students wrote a short summary or *review* of the information learned in the chapter. For PM2R, the students *previewed* the chapters to see what information they would be reading. They then *measured* the length of the chapters to help them divide the reading into smaller parts. Moreover, measuring the length of the chapters would help them determine the amount of time needed to read. While *reading*, the students highlighted, circled pertinent terms, or wrote marginal notes. Afterwards, they *recited* or wrote the information.

KWL required the students to preview the chapter and then create a worksheet with three columns. In the first column labeled *"know,"* the students wrote down what they all ready knew about the chapter topics. In the second column entitled *"want,"* the students wrote down questions pertaining to the information they would like to learn about from the reading. In the final column, the students wrote a summary of what they *"learned."*

With SPARCS, students *surveyed* the chapter before reading and *predicted* the organizational pattern the author used. Types of organizational patterns included compare and contrast, sequence, cause and effect, and definition. These patterns helped students pinpoint how the information or wording was being structured. As the students *read* each section of the chapter, they stopped to assess what they read, what new questions arose, how the ideas were organized, and what to predict for the next section. This was the *construction* phase of the reading strategy. Once they completed the reading, they graphically *summarized* the main ideas by creating concept maps, tree diagrams, and charts to illustrate the information.

MURDER, a socially oriented reading strategy, offered students the opportunity to work in pairs. The students established a *mood* and mindset to begin reading. They also decided who would play the role of the teacher and student for certain sections in the chapter. They then read to *understand* the information rather than memorize it. After reading a section, the student in the role of the teacher recited or taught that section to the other student. The goal for this stage of the strategy was to *recall* the information without using the text. The other student listened for or *detected* mistakes and asked questions. Once the teaching was done for a section, the two students *elaborated* on the important points to remember and devised possible test questions. Upon completion of the entire chapter, they *reviewed* the material to make sure that they covered it thoroughly. In addition, after a test, the students met again to discuss errors made on the test.

In short, these strategies got the students to do something before, during, and after the reading. Thus, presumably, the students became more active and critical readers. Furthermore, one of the strategies gave students the opportunity to work together as they learned the information.

In addition to learning strategies for reading, students were introduced to note-taking strategies such as SU/Cornell and Jeopardy (Blumin, 1997). For SU/Cornell, before the students took notes, they drew a vertical line two-and-one-half inches from the left margin. This area became their "recall" column. Two inches from the bottom of the page, they drew a horizontal line. The space below the horizontal line became their summary box. The large space above the summary box and next to the recall column was where the students took their notes as usual. After the lecture, the students read their notes and reduced them to key terms in the recall column. The key terms would help trigger the information on that page of notes. If their notes had gaps, they also had the opportunity to write down questions to ask of their professors individually or in the next lecture. Before the next lecture, the students wrote a brief summary of the information on each page of notes. This strategy was good for learning a lot of new information. Moreover, it was good for multiple-choice tests.

For the Jeopardy note-taking strategy, students only wrote their notes on the right side of the notebook. They took their notes in paragraph form, indented supporting details, skipped lines to separate information, and underlined or starred important points. After lecture, the students reread their notes and created questions from their notes on the other side of the notebook. Like the previous note-taking strategy, students would be able to identify gaps in their notes and ask questions of their professors individually or in lecture. This strategy was good for essay tests.

Both of these note-taking strategies acted as a test preparation tool, forcing the students to review their notes after lecture and not just before a test or an examination. Furthermore, study time would be reduced.

Students were also taught test-taking strategies (Blumin, 1994; Blumin, 1997). For example, they were taught to do a "Q and A" Map for old quizzes or examinations they had been given. Sometimes old tests were available at the reserve desk at BTU's main library. For this strategy, students divided a sheet of paper into several columns. In the left hand column, labeled "topics," students wrote down the major topics that appeared on the test. Next, they wrote the different types of organizational patterns in the other columns. Types of organizational patterns included "compare and contrast," "sequence," "cause and effect," and "definition." These patterns helped students pinpoint how the information or wording was structured on the test. Finally, students read through the test and placed a check mark next to the topic under a particular organizational pattern. This would help the student note the types of questions distributed throughout the test and to anticipate what to focus on for the next test.

In the Post Exam Analysis test-taking strategy, students reflected on how they took notes, read, anticipated possible test questions, studied with a friend, sought assistance from the professors, or used review sheets and old tests. Beyond this, they posed questions dealing with the time they allotted to study, their confidence level, and the easiest and hardest questions that appeared on the test. Based upon this analysis, the students would determine how to prepare for the next test. Even though a number of strategies were taught in the SSC courses, students were encouraged to alter them to fit their ways of learning.

In sum, the course was intended to (1) help students read critically and strategically to get the most out of assigned readings; (2) use strategic ways to study for examinations; (3) take analytical class notes when appropriate; (4) develop peer networks for studying; (5) develop ways of communicating with professors; and (6) help all students transition academically and socially into BTU. As the next sections show, few of these strategies made it into these Black students' repertoire.

4.2 THE AFTERMATH OF TAKING AN SSC COURSE: THE ACADEMIC TRANSITION

Unfortunately, the assumptions of the SSC teachers did not reflect the very real situations in which the students found themselves. Often, professors at BTU either ignored textbooks or simply paraphrased the information in them during lectures. Examinations were often based upon banks of test questions that were used from semester-to-semester. Interestingly, only one student, a former SSC undergraduate teaching assistant, used any of the SSC strategies in her courses. Another student applied a reading strategy, while the other used a note-taking strategy. As the following sections will show, a majority of the students fell back to their old ways of coping or surviving the demands of their academic course work at this predominantly White private university.

4.3 "A DIFFERENCE BETWEEN READING AND STUDYING"

The goals of the SSC reading strategies were to get students to do something before, during, and after reading. Thus, these strategies were intended to help students become more active rather than passive readers. However, even after taking an SSC course, Black students felt no need to use the reading strategies as long as they believed they could obtain their information from lecture. For example, Bryan, who tried reading his philosophy textbook with a friend during his freshman year, said,

> Um, I believe we have readings, but I don't have the book. . . .Because we don't really talk about readings in class. . . .Like each chapter has a group that has to present [a chapter] before the class. They go up and present and we just listen to them. You get the summary of the chapter.

Similarly, Imani evidenced the same behavior for one of her courses. She stated,

> . . . I don't read for that class because I don't think there's a need. I'll read when it comes time for the final because the final is on chapters in the book, but [the professor] goes over [the chapters] in class.

Imani also said that she did not buy the book for that class. Instead, she got it from one of the athletes in the class since "they get their books free."

It appeared that, if assigned readings were summarized by the professor or presented by the students during lecture, students like Bryan and Imani were not going to read. Even though the information discussed would not be thorough, it seemed to them that they would get what they needed to get by in the course. In addition, as these two seniors and the other students advanced through their college years, they became savvier in the sense of not buying books. They did this because as freshmen students, they had learned that the books they bought were not used in some of their courses.

As for Kenya, who struggled with reading the course material her first year at the university, the battle was still not won. For instance, in her religion class, she stressed,

> I just don't understand what they're talking about. . . .When I tried to read the book, I really couldn't understand [it]. I tried to read like line by line. Even when I did that at first, I'm like o.k. [Kenya] just try to weed out whatever you don't get and try to understand the basic concepts. I really just couldn't get pass the first page.

As a result of not comprehending the reading material, she resorted to obtaining her information from lecture as she did before. Unfortunately, Kenya said the lecture did not clear up her confusion because the professor was presenting his own thoughts on the topics. His lecture on the topics also went against her religious beliefs.

Hearing that Kenya was struggling with the reading, I asked if she had tried any of the reading strategies she learned in SSC. She stated that she created her own reading strategy by taking parts from the SSC reading strategies. That is, "I read the preface, summary, and heading to weed out the main points." However, because "the book was rigid and dry, I was not motivated to read it. [The] information was like Chinese." In addition, she asserted that since the book as well as the professor's lectures went against her religious beliefs, it was difficult for her to accept the information. Furthermore, "because time was of essence and [she] had other [course] work to do," she did not want to waste time on the religion course. Sadly, after not performing well on her midterm, she dropped the course; in her words, "I can't afford my GPA to suffer this semester. Everything is on the line." Nonetheless, dropping the religion course did not improve her GPA because Kenya was back on academic probation her junior year.

As a freshman, this young woman had shown great enthusiasm toward coming to BTU. However, after a while, her enthusiasm dissipated. In her words,

> . . . I really think that I would have been better off saving my money [by] going to the library at home and just reading all the books there . . . self educating myself, and probably attending some of the classes at a community college. Like I'm paying all this money. All this money and all these loans, and I'm like just

paying them to give me a certificate that says [Big Time University] on it. I'm trying my best to get whatever I can out of it. It's sad.

As a freshman, Darnell only read what was needed to write a paper for his writing class. Now, he was specifically reading for a physics test the day before the examination. He explained,

I couldn't skim [the chapters]. I read them. I read the chapters. I didn't study the chapters. There's a difference between reading and studying. . . . There are two times when you get a lot of your information, when it's crunch time and you're reading to get out and when you like it.

Darnell delayed reading for this course as well as some of the others because he "was not enthusiastic about the reading." Moreover, he only read the physics chapters because "I need[ed] to get this done" before the exam. Therefore, because it was the night before the test and the clock was ticking, he used his own reading strategy instead of an SSC strategy. He said he focused on

. . . the one sentence in the paragraph that actually describes what's going on in the paragraph. After that line, I have a very good idea what that paragraph is about. You know it's kind of like a pointer.

He also stated that he took fifteen-minute breaks while reading for the course. A friend influenced him to take these breaks when they studied for their engineering courses together. This was a big change from his freshman year because then he "read until [his] eyes hurt." He also pointed out that another reason he waited to read for the physics course was because it was not as important as his other engineering courses as far as the credit value. Even though Darnell's strategy appeared somewhat effective in terms of his grade, he still was reading out of desperation.

While Darnell read the book, Imani perused the chapters for her interviewing course the day before her test. She explained,

Before the midterm, we had to read like chapters 1 through 5. I asked one of my friends for the book. [I] looked over [the chapters, and I] looked over my notes. [I] didn't read.

When I asked her what her test grade was, she humorously remarked, "I got a 77, then [the professor] added 2 points and I got a 79. We did extra credit for 20 points so I have a 99 now (laughs). Extra credit for the midterm." The extra credit assignment required students to go out and conduct interviews. Imani, who only studied old chemistry examinations her freshman year, was jovial over her success, even though her grade was the result of extra credit and not critical reading. She also added that, since the professor discussed the reading in class, using an SSC reading strategy, which involved the assigned reading, was pointless.

Students continued reading for the purpose of writing papers. For instance, Larry wrote a paper for his office systems technology course the night before it was due. He said,

> Uh actually the paper was based on a chapter in the book. So, I just borrowed somebody's book and read the chapter and did the paper based on other things I know, implemented that and mixed it all together.

Larry had been successful in writing papers the night before or the same day that papers were due since he had come to BTU. He said "paper writing was the easiest because I wrote papers all in high school." In high school, he had written papers in his math and science courses rather than taking tests. Larry also pointed out that he received good grades on his papers at BTU before and after taking SSC. In short, Darnell, Imani, and Larry read or perused the assigned material only to complete an academic task for a grade.

While the other students failed to apply reading strategies, Stacy used the SSC reading strategy, PM2R, for her computer science class. As a freshman, she specifically read what she had to for examinations and assignments. Now, she said she knew she had to learn or thoroughly understand the definitions for her computer science course. Therefore, she said she previewed and measured the chapters. After each section within a chapter, she would make "margin notes or jot down key points after each paragraph." Later, she wrote a summary after reading the chapter. By doing this, she would not have to go back and reread the information. Although she did not begin reading for that class until after midterm, she pointed out that she did perform well in the course.

Even though Stacy was no longer an undergraduate teaching assistant (UTA) when she took this class, she was probably more apt to use a reading strategy because she had taught other SSC students how to use the strategies in their other courses. Furthermore, while an undergraduate teaching assistant (UTA), it was mandatory for her to attend all SSC lectures and the hands-on mentoring course. Therefore, she had the advantage of hearing the information a second time in lecture and discussing the strategies with other UTAs in the hands-on mentoring course.

Overall, the students' reading strategies had not changed much since the SSC course. They continued to read primarily for a test or an assignment. For those who did not read, they obtained their information primarily from lecture. Sadly, in Kenya's case, when the lecture or book did not help, she dropped the class. Unfortunately, the professors' practices did not encourage most of the students to read in ways beyond "getting by." Obviously, the students felt more comfortable using their past strategies since they had helped them to survive in an environment they perceived as alienating.

4.4 "I HATE READING,
BUT I READ A 500-PAGE BOOK IN THREE DAYS"

While the students only read for tests or papers, there were occasions when they read books that were relevant to them. Sometimes the books had nothing to do with the courses. For example, Darnell pointed out that he enjoyed reading books by Anne Rice. He stated, "I hate reading, but I read a 500 page book, [*Tale of the Body Thief*], in three days." He said that he liked the major character in the book because he was "a lot like me, or I think I'm a lot like him in the story [because] he doesn't like to follow rules." Darnell added that "anything where someone is breaking the rules and standing for what they believe in just captures my attention." Unfortunately, his course readings did not capture his attention like the Anne Rice novel.

Knowing that he read a book with 500 pages in three days amazed me because after his experience with a sociology course his first semester at BTU, he made a vow to never take another course that required a lot of reading again. I assumed that he hated reading. However, he clarified why the novel was so much better than his textbook:

> When you're enthusiastic about something, you just like gather it up. If I'm not feeling like I'm gathering it up, I tend to go back to make sure I'm getting it and sometimes I find myself reading the same paragraph four or five times. You want to know the worst thing about that, after reading it the fifth time; you're like 'I don't get it.'

Thus, he struggled with the assigned readings in courses like sociology that were not interesting to him and often gave up on reading altogether. It was quite clear that Darnell was capable of reading, since he read a book with 500 pages with no problem. The problem arose when he was not motivated to read in courses such as his sociology class.

While Darnell found pleasure in reading books outside the classroom, Imani enjoyed reading assigned books in her African-American Studies class. Regarding the book *Assata: An Autobiography* by Assata Shakur (1987), she remarked,

> It just caught my attention. . . .That was interesting to me because that's somebody who was in political exile in Cuba. It's just like gosh. She's living her life

[like that]. I could live my life like that. It made you want to learn more on why
she did what she did, and how she did it you know. It made me think if I were
in that situation, what would I do?

Imani took the survival experiences of the person in the book and connected them to real life. As a result, the book became more intriguing to her.
It was not tasteless reading but reading with flavor. She was able to savor the
words and read deeply. Students like Imani did not complain about reading
books in their African-American Studies course because the books compen-
sated for the personal involvement they were not getting in their other
courses. That is, the students stated that in most of their classes, they either
did not discuss Black issues or the professors merely "touched" on them.
Therefore, reading books in their African-American Studies courses gave
them the opportunity to see themselves in the pages and make a personal connection with the Black characters or situations. They also had the chance to
talk about the books as well as Black issues in the African-American Studies
class.

While still attempting to make the academic transition into BTU, students
like Imani often found other channels to compensate for what they were not
getting in their courses. As for Darnell, he sought readings that were exciting
and had characters that he believed were like him. It was when they used
these channels that they were motivated or encouraged to read. Because of
their enthusiasm for books they liked, they did not use any SSC reading
strategies. As the next section reveals, two students did use the SSC note-
taking strategies in their courses. The strategies themselves, however, were
not a guarantee of success.

4.5 "I USED JEOPARDY TO TAKE THE LECTURE NOTES"

The purpose of the SSC note-taking strategies was to motivate students to review their notes after lecture and not just before an examination. This would
reduce study time. In addition, by reviewing their notes, they would be able
to catch any gaps and therefore would be able to ask questions of their
professors or in lecture to obtain the needed information. While most of the
students resorted to taking notes as they had before, two of the students did
apply the SSC note-taking strategies to their other classes.

For example, Stacy applied the Jeopardy note-taking strategy in her adolescent psychology class. Unfortunately, she only received "Cs" on all of her
tests and got a "C" out of the course. I was curious about how she implemented the strategy. Thus, I asked her to explain what she did. She stated that

to prepare for the first test, she placed the questions she had formed from her class notes on flashcards. However, she did not review or form questions from her notes to create those flashcards until a few days before the test. Moreover, she did not dedicate enough time to study for the test because she was trying to prepare for an examination in another course. Apparently, she was not following all of the steps to the SSC note-taking strategy. Presumably, if she had allowed more time to study, reviewed her notes on a constant basis, and sought needed help from the professor, she might have done better. Nevertheless, Stacy "swore [she] knew the information in that class." In her words, "I could spit out the information. Maybe it was the way [the professor] phrased the questions on the test." She concluded "nothing could have helped me in that class."

Tina used the SU/Cornell note-taking strategy for her earth science class. However, she said that the strategy did help her "understand the information [even though] the professor did not teach the class proficiently." That is, "he would go off on tangents during the lecture." Knowing that her professor went off on tangents, Tina never went to him to clarify any possible gaps or inconsistencies in her lecture notes. She also did not review her notes on a constant basis. Like Stacy, she did not follow all the parts of the SSC note-taking strategy. Because her lecture notes did not coincide with the information on the midterm exam, she received a "D." As a result of getting a "D" on the midterm, she dropped the course and planned to take it again in the fall.

Obviously, these two students failed to implement all steps of the note-taking strategies, especially the social aspect of the strategies. Particularly, by failing to make these social connections, the note-taking strategies were of little assistance. Perhaps, because they were in an environment that they continued to perceive as alienating, they still did not feel comfortable going to professors for help. That is, Tina had stated, "for some reason, these professors intimidate me." Moreover, Stacy often commented that the student-teacher relationship was impersonal.

4.6 "DUH, GO PICK THE [OLD] EXAMS UP" AT THE RESERVE DESK

The goals of the SSC test-taking strategies were to help students focus on the distribution of questions on previous tests, anticipate possible test questions, allot study time, seek assistance, and so on. However, instead of using these SSC strategies to analyze old examinations, students used old tests on reserve at BTU's main library as they did previously. For example, Tina, whom I interviewed before her economics midterm, remarked that her test preparation focused on her homework and the old midterm tests on reserve. She pointed out that "all of [the old exams] coincided with each other." When her friends did not know how to prepare for the test she told them to "Duh, go pick the [old] exams up [at the reserve desk] and look at each exam. . . . If you see these three questions on all these exams, then you know he's going to ask these three questions." Initially, Tina believed that she did very well on the exam. Unfortunately, when I interviewed her after the exam, she confirmed that she did not perform well. She received a 43 on the examination and was devastated. Tina stated that the professor "switched the wording [on the midterm test], but it's the same concept [as that on the old tests]." She also said the test was "short answer with one big essay question." However, because she did not accurately answer the questions, she lost points. I asked her why she did not use the test-taking strategies learned in SSC. She replied, "I didn't think about them." Tina was confident that studying the old tests and using her homework would prepare her for the exam. Sadly, her economics test results were unlike the good test scores she received her freshman year when she only obtained information from lecture. As a result of her performance on the exam, she dropped the class and decided to take it the following semester.

Not all old examinations were on reserve at the main library. Some students used previous tests from the courses they were enrolled in for that semester. For example, Terrell, who only read to complete an assignment in his freshman year, now used his old tests in his geology course to help him pass the final examination for a course he was failing. He also sought help from his roommate. According to Terrell, his roommate had a way of determining which questions the professor would put on the test. Therefore, they went over the class notes and he memorized the questions and answers to the previous three tests. Terrell got a 99 on the test because "all [the professor] did was take the questions from his first 3 tests and just put them on the final. . . . He just arranged the order differently." By using this strategy, he brought his average up from an "F" to a "C." Because he was in jeopardy of failing the course, I wanted to know why Terrell did not use the SSC test-taking strategies to study for this final exam. He stated that "the problem was that I waited too long to study, so I crammed the night before." Terrell also became "so nervous" and desperate to pass the course that he was flunking until he resorted to a strategy that worked at that moment.

Other students acquired old exams from other students. For example, Darnell pointed out that engineering students were told to keep their old exams. Therefore, "if you need an exam or old homework, just go to someone you knew who took the class and nine times out of ten they have it." He further described how he used the old exams to prepare for his assembly language final:

I did all the problems on the exam. And if I didn't get the problems done, I would look at the way the person did it . . . . If they got something wrong, the professors would have corrected the part they got wrong. So, I would know how to do the problem. And it worked out perfectly because for my assembly [language] final, they had five problems. They chose the same five from the previous year. No, four of the five problems were the exact same problems with the exact same numbers, and ten minutes before [the test], I had already done those problems. (smiles) So I was just regurgitating everything I had done ten minutes prior. I went into the final with a "C," and I got a "B+" in the class. . . .That means I got an "A" on the final.

Even though they were not using the SSC strategies, both Terrell and Darnell did study the old examinations in a fairly sophisticated and purposeful way.

Stacy, on the other hand, did use the SSC test-taking strategies in her hardest course, adolescent psychology. Previously, she used her own strategy to study old Biology tests. Now, after not obtaining the grade she desired on her first adolescent psychology exam, she used the Q and A Map to analyze the test. For this strategy, she divided the sheet of paper into several columns. In the left hand column labeled "topics," she wrote down the major topics that appeared on her exam. In the other columns, she wrote down the different organizational patterns (compare and contrast, sequence, cause and effect, and so on). Next, she read through her exam and placed a check mark next to the topic under a particular organizational pattern. Unfortunately, using this strategy did not work because she received the same grade on her second exam. She "had no idea why it didn't work." However, it probably was not successful because she did not obtain immediate help from the professor.

Nevertheless, she did use the Post Exam Analysis test-taking strategy. This strategy enabled her to reflect on how she took notes, read, sought assistance, and so on. From that strategy, she concluded that she spent more time on questions at the beginning of the test than she did with the questions toward the end of the test. Therefore, she rushed through the later part of the test and lost more points.

Although using old tests to study did not help Tina, Terrell and Darnell were able to raise their grades to a "C" and "B+" respectively. The one student who did use the strategy was not significantly helped because she did not get assistance from the professor. Even though they had been taught a number of academic and social strategies in their SSC courses, they failed to use them, either because their professors taught in ways that did not encourage them to use the strategies, or because the environment was so alienating, their social circumstances impinged upon their academic lives.

4.7 BEYOND THEIR FRESHMAN YEAR AT BTU:
THE SOCIAL TRANSITION

After their freshman year, the social challenges or difficulties had not changed much for these students. Black males continued being perceived by many White students and staff as BTU athletes. However, Bryan, who first experienced this stereotype while registering for fall classes his freshman year, started using it to his advantage. He had not done well on the last two tests in one of his courses and needed to pass the next test to get the "credit to graduate." Therefore, after lecture, he decided to speak to his White professor. Nevertheless, before approaching the professor, a friend whispered, "Yo, tell her you play football." Bryan had heard that the professor was really nice to athletes and therefore took his friend's advice. Bryan, who was six foot four, approached his professor stating, "Can I meet with you after class?" "Sure, come to my office," replied the professor. He explained,

> She said, 'Do you play sports?' I was like yeah; I play football. She said, 'Oh really, what [position] do you play?' I was like well really I'm a walk-on. . . . She told me to come meet with her and she would help me with the test and give me more studying [material]. . . . There are two dates you can take the test. So, I'm going to take it on the second day.

Bryan, who often failed to attend class, was able to get the help he needed two weeks before the test without being scorned by the professor. While Bryan used this stereotype to get the help needed, there were other stereotypes that these Black students found to be very disrespectful. For example, Larry described a social event that took place among White students.

> . . . These um white fraternities and sororities had some party called quote un-quote ghetto party. You had to dress like you were quote   unquote ghetto or you couldn't get in or something like that. I wish I had seen a flyer; I would have went to the party. But of course people don't really hear about things like this. You know it's real secretive. I wish I could have heard something like that.

Obviously, Larry learned to believe that when most White people use the word "ghetto," they equated it with minorities.

These students also responded to the Sambo image of the Black Student Government Association President that was published in the student newspaper. The newspaper, *Voices Heard*, was criticizing the SGA's alleged misuse of funds when it portrayed the SGA President as dark-skinned with "enlarged facial features and large hands" (Selvam, 1999, p. 1). Students retaliated by rallying in front of the newspaper's office and carrying signs with a blown-up version of the image and a caption reading, "[V. H.] Do you think this is funny? So funny we forgot to laugh. After 100 years, why is oppressive, stereotypical propaganda still humorous?" (p. 4). Imani expressed her frustration:

> I was really upset. . . . I was like this really is a Sambo-type picture. I couldn't believe they did it. . . . I was telling my mother the other day, I was like 'I am experiencing racism first hand and I thought [BTU] was about diversity and this that and the third.' I was like 'I can't believe this.'

Imani was dissatisfied with the apology the student newspaper wrote the next day. In fact, she used the pronoun "me" to include herself in this situation. The degradation of this incident was no longer pertaining to the Black SGA President but to her too. She stressed, "I mean the apology [the newspaper] gave to me was crap that they did the next day. It wasn't really like a real apology." Similarly, Larry, who participated in the student rally, found the apology bogus. He affirmed,

> The [newspaper staff] apologized but they were laughing under their breath. I just want to know [why] they didn't have no answers? That's what I wanted to know, why? What was going through your mind? You were just going to put this in here and everybody was going to sit here and laugh about it with you. I mean maybe that's the reflection or I guess the audacity that individuals still have. Maybe something drastic needs to happen, not necessarily physical. I mean it's (racism) there. Racism is definitely there.

The insensitivity and disrespect of these situations were just more examples that illustrated why Black students would feel uncomfortable and alienated on this predominantly White private campus. These situations also showed the type of environment the students were trying to survive.

Tina shared her perception of how Black students were treated differently than White students when it came to obtaining permission to hold a social event on campus. She pointed out,

> I just feel like they treat us differently than they treat the Caucasians. Also, I don't feel it's a fair type of thing because it seems like everybody I talk to that's on different organizations, they have to go through so much just to get something, you know, done. And when [Black students] get something done, it's at the last minute because [the university staff] waited until the last minute to let them, you know, know if they can do it.

She explained the difference between how Whites and Blacks were treated by adding,

From what I've heard, when [White students] put something in, two or three weeks later, they get an answer. Blacks students, they put something in a month ago [but] still haven't heard nothing back. So it's like, I don't know, it's frustrating to some [Blacks], but at the same time a lot of them be like 'whatever.' That's why a lot of [Black] people don't like to put in the effort to get things done because it takes so long for [the university staff] to go through the changes.

According to Tina, the university staff appeared to ignore the Black students more and favored the White students. In her mind, members of the university staff held a hidden stereotype when her Black friends sought permission to hold a social event on campus.

Besides stereotypes and racism, these students continued feeling the stigma of being the only Black student in the classroom. For example, Stacy pointed out that being the only Black in the classroom made her "feel like [she was] in competition with [White students]. I feel like they already have an advantage you know." In addition, she asserted,

Like the [White] girls in my major, I don't talk to them [about my grades]. I don't want [White] people to get any preconceptions, you know, like when they ask exactly how I'm doing [in my courses]. I say I'm doing fine. Even if I'm not, you don't need to know. You see what I'm saying?

She continued, "I feel I have to work like ten times harder [than they do]. I don't know why. I really don't know why but (pause) I know I feel I do."

Even though students like Stacy felt estranged in their classes, students who took the SSC summer seminar course felt comfortable because they were in a learning environment where a majority of the students and instructor was Black. For example, Kenya explained,

I really loved that class. I felt free to express myself. It was really cool. My confidence level rose because if I said something I wasn't attacked. . . . I felt free to talk about issues I was learning. . . . We were able to be ourselves.

The SSC summer class appeared to have offered students like Kenya something they had not experienced at BTU. That is, they were in a class where they were not only in the majority but she was not dealing with alienation. Unfortunately, this experience was not prevalent in their other courses.

These Black students continued to encounter alienation, racism and stereotypes on this predominantly White campus. Therefore, because they did not accept the disrespectful behavior from White students and teachers, their social transition into BTU was not complete. Considering the competition and marginalization they felt, perhaps it was not surprising that they were in a constant state of panic to pass examinations, used only parts of SSC strategies, and failed to make important social connections that would allow them to succeed.

4.8 THE CURRICULUM: "I FEEL LIKE I'M LEFT OUT"

Unfortunately, if students did not take an African-American Studies course, learning and voicing their opinions about a Black issue was a rare opportunity in some of the classes they took. When I asked these students if their professors included Black issues in some class topics, they either remarked that the professors merely "touched on it" or that Black issues were not discussed at all. To compensate for the lack of attention to Black issues in some of his courses, Larry said, "I made everything relate to me, man. Like any class that I take . . . . I made it relative to myself." For example, to understand a theory during his philosophy class, he applied it to life in his inner-city neighborhood:

> I mean there are certain parts of New York City that aren't um I guess as safe as others. So, there's been plenty of times which I had to decide which way in which I was going to take, depending on what situation . . . . All right, if I come to an avenue and it's 114th street and 113th street, I have to decide which way I want to go. And I know 114th street is safe and I believe 113th street might be safe; which way am I going to go? I'm going where I know. That example right there just went to the argument on the concept between knowledge and belief— which one is better?

Because of the scarce opportunities to discuss Black issues in the classroom, Tina said, "I feel like they deprive us because I guess it's generally just based on Caucasians." Kenya remarked that "[the professors were] not sensitive to my being an African American, my being an African American in the class." Similarly, Imani remarked, "I feel like I'm left out. I'm left out." As an example she stated,

> . . .like I remember this one specific time we were doing something in our speech communication class, and we had to watch some news shows. And I was like what happened to BET (Black Entertainment Television) um tonight and what happened to um you know um, what is that show, some show on MTV (Music Television) that was a Black show. I was like you know what's going on, why are you leaving out all the Black shows? My professor was like, "Oh I wasn't meaning to do that." But [he] said it, you know. So I was like, little stuff like that. They don't care.

It was obvious that the professor did not take into consideration the different racial and ethnic groups in his class. Moreover, he did not research or seek out ethnic news shows that were televised. As a result of his forgetfulness or unconsciousness, Imani became upset instead of enthusiastic or interested in the lesson.

Kenya reflected on a moment when a White professor was leading a discussion on how East Germans were being treated by West Germans. She explained that such words as prejudice, discrimination, and the economical issues in Germany paralleled the experiences of African Americans in America. Moreover, the discussion on the Holocaust in Germany made her think about the genocide that occurred during slavery. Even though she immediately saw the connections, the professor and students appeared to ignore them. Therefore, she took it upon herself to guide the discussion in that direction. Nevertheless, when she presented the comparisons of the two situations, the professor "briefly agreed with [her]. He said, 'Yes, but in East Germany. . .,' he went back to Germany."

The professor's response hurt her because he did not give any considerations to her observations. Kenya stated, "It was no way that someone could walk into that classroom knowing, you know, the current events of this nation and not think it's parallel." Not willing to give up, Kenya said she "waited for the opportunity to again resurrect the similarity" of the two situations. Unfortunately, once more the professor "briefly agreed and then again he went back to East Germany." She remarked,

> After class, he came up to me and he said, "I thank you for bringing that up because that's what I wanted to get people thinking of, but I didn't want to say it. I wanted people to bring it up." But then, I didn't mention it to him, but I was thinking, 'Why didn't you stay on the topic?' Why is it every time that I mentioned the plight of African Americans in this country and the effects of slavery, and you know the economic and discrimination turmoil that's going on now, you know; I'm thinking, 'why didn't you stay on that topic?' So, I didn't even bother asking. I left it alone and just shook my head.

Kenya walked out of the class that day disappointed that her professor ignored her observation. Moreover, he silenced her voice because he continued with his lecture. From Kenya's vantage point, her professor was afraid to discuss the topic. In addition, because of this experience, Kenya said she was reluctant to approach him. She stated that she would only go to him to obtain assignments. When she needed help, she went to the teaching assistant.

On the rare occasions when these students were able to discuss issues that pertained to Blacks, they took the opportunity to set the record straight on some topics. For example, Bryan said that a White student gave a speech on "how they should take away affirmative action." He pointed out that she apparently "didn't really see like the importance of affirmative action." The student "was coming off a viewpoint like um a close friend's father of hers didn't get a sergeant position in a district. A Black guy did because of affirmative action." Bryan asked her, "How many Black people do you think would actually be here [at BTU] if affirmative action wasn't here?" The student responded by stating that she did not know. It was perhaps understandable for Bryan and the White student to view affirmative action differently. While he viewed it as an opportunity for a deprived race, she saw it as reverse discrimination. Kravitz and Plantania (1993) showed that affirmative action was a misconstrued term. "Instead of viewing affirmative action as a defense against discrimination, affirmative action is often referred to as a perpetrator of discrimination" (Sax & Arredondo, 1996).

In another example, Tina's critical issues class, where she was the only Black student, was given an in-class group assignment to read profiles of students who applied to the university. They also had to decide whether or not these students should be admitted into BTU. Tina's group focused on a Black, female high school student who had to balance schoolwork and the responsibilities at home. Tina explained that this student's "mother was working 50 plus hours a week." As a result, the student, who maintained a 3.0 GPA, took care of her younger brothers and sisters, cooked, and cleaned the family's home in addition to going to school. Tina emphasized that

> with all the distractions that [student] had taking care of home [responsibilities], her [high school] recommendation said that she did more than her share of the work. Like if they gave her an assignment, she did more then what that assignment asked.

Unfortunately, a White student, who constantly bragged that his father was a doctor, did not take any of this into consideration. According to Tina, he said, "Well, I don't think she should be included into the [BTU] community because um she doesn't have much community service." In defense of the female student, Tina stressed to the White student that the young woman's home and school responsibilities proved that she was a very competent person. She accentuated that "any person who can go to school for 8 hours, come home, clean and watch kids, cook and plus do homework is a very high strung person." Moreover, she asserted,

> some of us come home from school and just lay around. I mean we don't have to clean. We don't have to watch our little sisters and brothers. We don't have to help our mother do this that and the other because it's already done or there's somebody there to do it.

Furthermore, Tina made it clear to the White student that everyone did not come from the same background as he, and he had to take that into consideration. The student sighed and rolled his eyes at her remarks.

Apparently, in order for their White classmates to see the other side of particular issues, these Black students, who were the racial minority in the classroom, bore the representative burden of "educating" Whites on the Black experience. Feagin, Vera, and Imani (1996) pointed out that Black students often had to become "defenders" and "explainers" of their race (p. 91). Even though they did not want to become spokespersons for an entire race, they were forced to do so in certain situations in order to eliminate stereotypical beliefs and to get White students to view situations through the eyes of another race.

Occasionally, the alienation in the curriculum at BTU led these students to compensate by making the course material relevant to themselves. Moreover, the lack of attention to Black issues in the curriculum not only offended these Black students but caused them to believe that their White classmates were allowed to remain uneducated. Thus, academically, as well as socially, the students in the study did not appear to make a complete transition into the BTU environment.

4.9 SEEKING ACADEMIC HELP:
"FOR SOME REASON, THESE PROFESSORS INTIMIDATE ME"

Not surprisingly, given the alienation and marginalization that these students felt from many of their White professors, seeking assistance was not an easy decision to make. For example, as Stacy pointed out, she initially preferred to "handle [problems in the course] on [her] own. I can say like I did bad on this [test], but I'll do better you know. If I don't do well on the next one, then I'll go get help. So it's more like I guess I feel like I can do it on my own." Stacy used the adolescent psychology course mentioned previously as an example of this analogy. After receiving a "C" on her first and second adolescent psychology tests, Stacy got a tutor. She stated that the tutor was helpful, but because she waited "like two weeks before the final exam" to get one, she received a "C" in the course. Earlier, it was also shown that Stacy used an SSC note-taking strategy for this course. However, because she used only one part of the strategy and failed to seek help earlier, the strategy did not work. Perhaps, if Stacy had implemented the strategy correctly and then sought immediate assistance from the professor, she would have done better. As in her freshman year, Stacy continued going to other Black students for help rather than the professor. Terrell used the same reasoning as Stacy, but instead of a tutor, he went to another student for help in preparation for his geology final. Nevertheless, he said he sought assistance from professors in some of his courses, even though it was not immediate.

Before dropping her economics class, Tina did go to the professor for assistance. Unfortunately, the professor was "always in and out. So, by the time I was trying to get to him, it was the last day to drop." When I asked her why she did not seek help prior to taking the midterm exam, she said she was not having any problems at the time. As in her freshman year, students like Tina continued to drop courses when they experienced difficulties.

Even though Tina did not seek immediate help from her White professor, she had no difficulties going to her Black African-American Studies teacher to discuss her score on a test. She believed that "Black professors have more higher expectations for African-American students and are more upfront with [them]."

Going to the professor continued to be a difficult task for these students. Rather than seeking immediate assistance from professors, they sought help from teaching assistants, peers, or tutors. This behavior may have developed because they were in an environment that has alienated them since they first arrived on BTU's campus.

In sum, even though the students took a study skills course at BTU, they still were not able to transition fully into this alienating environment academically or socially. Academically, the assumptions of the SSC instructors did not hold true because professors taught in haphazard ways that rendered the strategies useless. That is, some professors either summarized the readings in class or did not use the books at all. The readings also did not often relate to these students' lives or racial background, so they were not motivated to read.

Second, while a majority of the students continued taking their notes as before, the two students who used the note-taking strategies were not particularly successful. They failed to follow all of the steps to the strategies and did not seek immediate assistance. When students were placed into situations where they were desperate or in a state of panic to pass a test or course, they often simply memorized old examinations. Sometimes the professors did not change previous examinations.

Finally, while the students made little or no use of academic strategies to help them in their reading, note taking, and test preparation, they also rarely used the social networking technique suggested by their SSC instructors. Perhaps the stereotypes, racism, and exclusion from the mainstream made them reluctant to approach professors.

When academic advisors recommended the SSC courses or the Student Development Program (SDP) made it mandatory for these students to take

SSC, they assumed that it would ameliorate the challenges these Black students were experiencing at this university. However, they failed to recognize the extent to which the social experiences exacerbated the academic experiences of these students. Therefore, it was likely that the SSC strategies alone were not significant to ameliorate the larger social and academic issues faced by these students in a predominantly White private institution.

Chapter Five

Conclusion, Recommendations, and Implications for Future Research

In review, the literature on study skills courses or programs at colleges and universities showed that these courses had been very beneficial to all students (Blanc, Debuhr, & Martin, 1983; Fidler & Hunter, 1989; Giles-Gee, 1989; Reis, 1989; Spitzberg & Thorndike, 1992; Stupka, 1993; Townsend, 1994). Although the courses or programs were beneficial to Black students, studies in this area were few (Giles-Gee, 1989; Spitzberg & Thorndike, 1992; Townsend, 1994). There were not any current studies that obtained Black students' perceptions on whether or not these courses aided in their social and academic integration into the academic mainstream.

Acquiring the students' perceptions on this issue was important because previous research illustrated that Black students had experiences that made integrating into predominantly White universities difficult (Allen, 1987; Allen, 1992; Bello-Ogunu, 1997; Fleming, 1984; Love, 1993; Nottingham, Rosen, & Parks, 1992; Philip, 1993; Phelon-Rucker, 2000; Turner, 1994; Willie & McCord, 1972). In addition, research showed that some Black students came from inner city high schools that lacked competitive and motivational environments (Richardson, Simmons, & Santos, 1987), and they were often academically underprepared (Allen, 1988; Jacobi, 1991; O'Brien, 1989; Pounds, 1987; Slater, 1994/1995; Tinto; 1987; Tinto, 1993; Wright, 1987). Thus, the high school experiences of Black students often led to a disjuncture between their previous school experiences and those in predominantly White environments (Allen, 1988; Love, 1993; Richardson, Simmons, and Santos, 1987; Tinto; 1987; Tinto, 1993).

In light of these situations, this qualitative study focused on the perceptions of a group of Black students who took study skills courses and the experiences they faced at a predominantly White private institution, when compared with their previous schooling experiences. In addition, this research presented the strategies and techniques the students talked about using prior to taking a study skills course. This study also concentrated on whether the study skills courses played a role in the students' academic and social integration into BTU once completed.

Tinto's (1993) theory of student departure, which was comprised of three stages: separation, transition, and incorporation, was the framework for this study. Tinto pointed out that in various settings, these stages would be repeated, partially completed, or overlapped. In this study, the Black students who took a study skills course did not make a complete transition nor incorporate into BTU in terms of social and academic integration.

5.1 SOCIAL TRANSITION

D'Augelli and Hashberger (1993) pointed out that when African-American students arrived on predominantly White campuses, they were coming from high schools and communities where they were in the majority. Findings from this study revealed that because most of these Black students were coming from high schools where they were in the racial majority, they had difficulties separating from their all-inclusive high school environments and transitioning into a predominantly White private university their freshman year. Moreover, in support of D'Augelli and Hashberger's (1993) research, one problem encountered was that a majority of the students in this study did not know many Black students when they arrived on BTU's campus first semester. Even when students like Terrell participated in BTU's summer Pre-College Program, a program aimed at easing the transition for minority students, they had problems separating from past, comfortable environments and transitioning into another.

In Terrell's case, he did not know or feel an immediate social connection with the other students in the Pre-College Program. Terrell had not come with anyone he knew, and therefore, even his encounters with other minority students also new to BTU were not particularly helpful in facilitating his transition. Dr. Brown, the director/professor of the study skills courses, commented,

> Well, that's interesting because that can be then why their isolation is intensified, because maybe White students come with their posse . . . whereas the Black students don't come with their support. . . . Remember how [the White kids seemed to be] all from the same block or from the same high school? . . . the Black students tend to be more independent and come alone. . . .[T]hat makes their transition different from the transition experience of White students.

In addition, she pointed out,

> It was very normal for [any] kid to come to a large university and feel over-whelmed. The fact that their teachers are not their neighbors anymore and their teachers are not available, and they don't see their teachers in the grocery store anymore, those are things that regardless of what color you are or who you are, that's a transitional issue.

However, she added that with Black students, their situation or experience is "accentuated by certain things" such as a limited number of Black professors and administrators on campus.

The students also experienced barriers or problems where they were often one of few Blacks on the same floor in dormitories. These living arrangements left many of them lonely, isolated, alienated, and distraught. For three of the Black male students, they had to deal with stereotypes where class-mates and university personnel perceived them as only coming to the univer-sity to play a sport rather than as students who wanted to get an education. Being lonely, isolated, alienated, dissatisfied with the environment, and con-tending with racism were psychosocial stressors that the students had to deal with at this predominantly White private university. Therefore, this study con-curred with the findings of previous studies (Allen, 1987; Allen, 1992; Bello-Ogunu, 1997; Fleming, 1984; Love, 1993; Nottingham, Rosen, & Parks, 1992; Philip, 1993; Phelon-Rucker, 2000; Turner, 1994; Willie & McCord, 1972) that showed psychosocial stress as being prevalent in the experiences of Black students at predominantly White institutions.

Succeeding at this predominantly White private university academically caused students like Larry to wonder or question if his high school had pre-pared him well. This apprehensiveness not only caused fear for failure, but it also became an added stress for some students.

As students tried to make the transition into BTU their freshman year, they began to experience what it felt like being the only Black student and voicing their opinions in the classroom. Their status as a "distinct minority" (D'Augelli & Hashberger, 1993) was again being reinforced for these stu-dents. They also appeared uncomfortable approaching their professors, espe-cially in their first semester. Instead, when they did seek help, they went to other students or the teaching assistants (TAs). Perhaps, the reason was that their White professors appeared more authoritative and intimidating than their TAs and peers. In high school, they did not have this problem. They used terms such as "nurturing," "concerned," "supportive," and they "knew your name" to describe the relationships with their high school teachers. It was not until the second semester that some students approached their professors and even then, this was the exception rather than the rule.

Even though the majority of the students in this study matriculated into the university in good standing from high schools where they were in the racial majority, it was obvious that the alienating environment took a toll on them as they tried to transition into a predominantly White university. According to Dr. Brown, "The academic transition is sometimes not the problem. It's the environmental transition the high school has not prepared [the students] for" that becomes challenging. This aspect of the study supports a national finding cited by Allen (1988) which revealed that Black students who attended high schools where they were in the majority were not prepared for the reality of being a racial minority in the predominantly White academic environment.

Beyond their freshman year and after taking an SSC course, students continued to witness the unconscious actions of professors, racism, stereotypes, being left out of the curriculum, and so on. They also still had difficulties going to their professors for immediate help. Although the SSC teachers encouraged students to go to their professors, the Black students in this study continued obtaining assistance from their peers and TAs. Apparently, the alienation and marginalization they had experienced previously made them seek help with people who were less intimidating. Because of the difficulties the students experienced inside and outside the classroom during their freshman year and beyond, these "guests at the ivory tower" had not made a complete social or academic transition.

Findings, in terms of Tinto's theory, suggest that the separation stage meant that the Black students in this study would have to change their lives and "check their former badges of power at the door" (Goldblatt, 1995, p. 27) of the ivory tower in order to fit into the university structure. Not surprisingly, "all too often [predominantly White] institutions expect [these] students to change while they continue business as usual, projecting an attitude that minority students should feel lucky that they are admitted" (Phillip, 1993, p.25). Perhaps if these universities made a greater effort to accommodate their unique needs, Black students would not feel the pressures of trying to adjust and fit into this environment. Moreover, they would not feel like trespassers in a strange land. Furthermore, because their social experiences impinged upon their academic experiences, the separation and transition stages for the Black students in this study were even more challenging and stressful during their freshman year and beyond.

5.2 RECOMMENDATIONS FOR SOCIAL TRANSITION

Although academic skills often receive the most attention in programs designed to assist racial minority students, this study suggests that universities should pay more attention to the social aspect of the integration process. First, more university outreach programs should be geared toward secondary schools where there are large minority populations. These programs can focus on preparing students who may attend a PWI or PWPI with the needed information and support to integrate socially and perform well academically. Contact personnel with university outreach programs should establish relationships with the students while the students are acquiring information and deciding whether or not to attend their university and after the students have made a decision to come to that university. Having a personal relationship with a contact person will ensure the students that they know someone on campus who they can go to in times of difficulty. Second, Love (1993) and Bello-Ogunu (1997) have argued that establishing multicultural training for institutional leadership is vital for transforming exclusionary predominantly White campuses into inclusive campuses. Training for this group is particularly important because most of the senior leaders received their training at predominantly White institutions "during an era when it was assumed that most Blacks would not attend PWIs" (Love, 1993, p. 33).

Bello-Ogunu (1997) also proposes that multicultural diversity training workshops and seminars be conducted often with students, faculty, staff, and especially residence halls staff. These workshops could stress values and methods of implementing diversity on campus, dealing with hate and interracial tension and improving multicultural relations (Bello-Ogunu, 1997). In addition, increasing the number of Black residence halls leaders could be very beneficial (Townsend, 1994).

Finally, researchers point out that "faculties must make sure that the materials and language they use fairly and effectively represent the various cultural, societal, and historical aspects of the subjects being taught" (*The Inclusive University*, 1993, p. 53). This teaching strategy could help all students appreciate other cultures besides their own (*The Inclusive University, 1993*) and "ensure that no single ideology silences the voices of others" (Phelon-Rucker, 2000, p. 90).

5.3 THE ROLE OF THE STUDY SKILLS COURSES IN THE ACADEMIC TRANSITION

Tinto (1993) pointed out that study skills programs had been one means of transitioning students into the social and academic environment of a university. Before taking a study skills course, the students used various unproductive strategies for reading, test-taking, and note-taking to transition academically and survive at this predominantly White private university. They rarely participated in in-depth reading of course material except when they had to prepare for specific tests, papers, and projects. Apparently, the students saw little personal connection with the assigned reading and rarely engaged in sophisticated reading strategies; instead they seemed to read perfunctorily to get a grade or to "get by." However, students did engage in reading when the material was relevant to them. One of the students found the assigned readings in her African-American Studies class as a form of "therapy." As for studying old tests, some students used the tests strategically while others simply memorized the answers to the tests—an approach with little or no value to them. Obviously, some students believed that studying old tests would help them succeed or "get by" in their courses. As for note taking, the students either tried to analyze the course information for an understanding or they only copied notes from the board. When the strategies they used were not effective, some students solved their academic problem by dropping the class.

It is important to note, however, that lack of study skills was only part of a much greater obstacle to the successful incorporation of these students into the university. Many social issues mentioned earlier seemed to have contributed to a state of constant distress during their freshman year and beyond. Because they had to deal with these issues and others, they were placed under a lot of pressure to perform well in a new learning environment. Therefore, they resorted to using strategies that would help them survive in this alienating environment. In short, because of the many social and academic challenges the students had to face at BTU, they had not made a complete academic nor social transition and did not reach Tinto's (1993) incorporation or integration stage during their freshman year. Furthermore, they were still trying to separate from their past learning environments.

The students eventually took one of the Study Skills for College Courses. However, students continued to fall back upon the same strategies they had used previously. That is, given that professors summarized readings, did not use textbooks, and did not often change tests from one semester to another seemed to cause the students to avoid using the strategies taught in the study skills courses. The teaching styles of many professors seemed to encourage them to continue taking short cuts and reinforced their notions of "getting by." Thus, a great deal of anxiety, coupled with what seemed like an alienating environment made the students feel under much pressure to do only what was necessary to perform well.

When some students used the SSC strategies, they left out important parts, particularly that of seeking immediate assistance from professors. Thus, the strategies were less effective than they might have been. Perhaps the marginalization and alienation they continued to experience caused them to avoid some professors. Therefore, although previous research showed that Black students generally benefited from study skills courses and programs (Giles-Gee, 1989; Spitzberg & Thorndike, 1992; Townsend, 1994), the remarks of Black students in this study indicated that they had difficulties fully integrating socially and academically into BTU, even after taking the SSC courses. Consequently, in terms of Tinto's theory, the learning strategies taught in the SSC courses alone were not sufficient to help the students make a complete academic and social transition into BTU.

Although a majority of the students did not use the SSC strategies, they reported having enjoyed their experience with the SSC courses. First, the courses got students to engage in meta-cognition. That is, they encouraged students to reflect on how they read, took notes and studied for tests, and then asked that they try other options such as using the SSC strategies. Students were also told that they could alter the strategies to fit their learning styles. Second, the SSC strategies encouraged social networking. Although the students did not interact with their professors as much as they should have, they did interact with their peers, tutors, and teaching assistants.

Finally, the students had a place on campus where they would go when they had a problem in their courses. As an instructor, I remembered having a few students return for advice on how to understand the concepts in difficult courses and which elective courses to take for the following semester. Sometimes, I became a sounding board for some students when they were dealing with personal problems. However, despite these benefits, Darnell, who took the summer seminar SSC course, asserted, "I don't think doing a small or bit program can prepare you for four years [of college]." Apparently, students like Darnell saw that SSC courses were not enough to survive or succeed at BTU.

5.4 RECOMMENDATIONS FOR ACADEMIC TRANSITION

University personnel should understand that a program to assist racial minorities in making the transition to a predominantly White university cannot be marginalized into one study skills course. A comprehensive program should be a university-wide effort, with dialogue occurring among professors, study skills instructors, and university administrators. During staff development meetings, discussions should focus on how to make academic expectations clearer on ways for inviting students to seek out professors for assistance. Students should also be involved in all phases of staff development.

Study skills teachers might want to create workshops for professors so that they can become more informed about the various strategies the course teaches. Perhaps, knowing about the study skills strategies may encourage professors to reinforce them in their courses. Study skills course instructors might also want to involve students in the design of these courses. Furthermore, instructors should consider making these courses longitudinal by having "check-in" seminars throughout the students' academic careers.

Perhaps a support system of learning (Spitzberg & Thorndike, 1992) can also be established. That is, a gathering place might be created on campus where Black students can have regular study sessions and obtain help from tutors. In addition, professors could participate in this support system. As is the case in the University of Virginia, professors might set up workshops in this gathering place to discuss course topics (Townsend, 1994). This could be very helpful for students who are having problems in the most challenging courses. Furthermore, having professors attend and participate in these workshops could be beneficial to Black students because they might not be as intimidated by White professors. Moreover, better student-professor relationships may lead Black students to find mentors. This type of program could provide these students with the social networks they need to perform well at a predominantly White university. As Spitzberg and Thorndike (1992) emphasize, minority students who have remained at universities often rely on supportive environments to help them excel in the academic mainstream. Knowing about such a source of support early in their academic career might give them the assurance that they will have the help needed to succeed.

5.5 IMPLICATIONS FOR FUTURE RESEARCH

Future research should be conducted in several areas. First, as a continuation of this study, Tinto's theory could be enriched further by conducting a more in-depth longitudinal study focusing on the perceptions of Black students who take study skills courses at predominantly White institutions, in terms of their social and academic integration. Second, research can also focus on Black students' involvement in the retention and recruitment process at predominantly White universities. Next, research pertaining to learning communities on university campuses is needed. Moreover, studies could explore how professors' stated expectations contrast with their teaching practices. The perceptions of racial minority students in these classes should be obtained. In addition, future studies might concentrate on the ways in which racially mixed high schools prepare their students for college. Furthermore, comparative studies concerning students from different racial groups, social classes, universities, and their degree of high school preparation seems warranted. Finally, conducting studies on White students who attend predominantly Black universities should be investigated in respect to Tinto's theory.

In terms of methods, study skills instructors can collaboratively conduct action research as they teach the courses. Individuals who are not study skills instructors such as outside researchers or peer ethnographers could also do future studies. As ethnographers, students such as those who take study skills courses can collect data that focus on their academic and non-academic settings. Furthermore, more studies using large-scale surveys on racism at predominantly White universities should be done.

It is important that predominantly White universities begin to devise programs that will allow Black students to have more positive academic and social experiences. As pointed out by Feagin, Vera, and Imani (1996), integration for Black students at predominantly White institutions is not a one-way street. Full integration for these students at such institutions has to be a two-way street with both parties taking on responsibilities (Feagin, Vera, & Imani, 1996). Perhaps then, Black students may not feel like "intruders in white territory" (Feagin, 1996, p.62) but as members of a learning community.

Appendices

A. INTERVIEW QUESTIONS—STUDENTS

Personal Background

____ What year are you in your program?
____ What is your major?
____ Where are you from?
____ Do you have any siblings?
____ Did your parents attend college?
____ How would you describe your family's economic status?
____ Could you describe your high school experience?
____ What was your high school GPA?

Freshman Year—Phase I

____ What was your first impression of the university?
____ Were there any stereotypes you experienced when you got here? If
so, what were they?
____ What were your first impressions of the large lectures?
____ What type of courses did you take first semester? Second semester?
____ How did you read for _____ course?
____ How did you take notes in _____ course?
____ How did you prepare for _____ exams?
____ What was the grade on the exams?
____ Were you going to your professors for help?
____ What was your GPA for the first semester? Second semester?

Beyond Freshman Year—Phase II

_____ What is it like being a Black student on this campus now?
_____ What type of courses are you taking now?
_____ How are you reading for _____ course?
_____ How are you taking notes in _____ course?
_____ How are you preparing for _____ exams?
_____ What was the grade on the exams?
_____ Are you going to your professors for help?

B. INTERVIEW QUESTIONS—DIRECTOR/PROFESSOR OF THE STUDY SKILLS FOR COLLEGE COURSES

_____ When was the first study skills course created?
_____ What was the structure of that course?
_____ When was SSC 101 created?
_____ What was the purpose of SSC 101?
_____ What is its benefits?
_____ Why were instructors and undergraduate teaching assistants added?
_____ What do you think students take away from this course?
_____ When was SSC 100 created?
_____ What was the purpose of SSC 100?
_____ What is its benefits?
_____ What do you think students take away from this course?

References

Allen, W. R. (1987). Black colleges vs. white colleges: The fork in the road for black students. *Change, 19*(3), 28–34.

———. (1988). The education of black students on white college campuses: What quality the experience? In Michael T. Nettles (Ed.) *Toward black undergraduate student equality in American higher education.* New York: Greenwood.

———. (1992). The color of success: African-American college student outcome at predominantly white and historically black public colleges and universities. *Harvard Educational Review, 62* (1), 26–44.

Arno, K. (1987). *The only game in town: Athletes-at-risk.* Unpublished doctoral dissertation, Syracuse University, Syracuse.

Bello-Ogunu, J. O. (1997). The problem of black students retention at white universities: Fabulous financial-aid package—not the answer. In Alicia King Redfern (Ed.), *Journal of the Pennsylvania Black Conference on Higher Education* (ERIC Document Reproduction Service No. ED420293)

Bender, D. S. (1997, February). *Effects of study skills programs on the academic behaviors of college students.* Paper presented at the meeting of the Annual Meeting of the Eastern Educational Research Association, Hilton Head, SC.

Blanc, R. A., Debuhr, L. E., & Martin, D. C. (1983). Breaking the attrition cycle: The effects of supplemental instruction on undergraduate performance and attrition. *Journal of Higher Education, 54,* 80–90.

Blumin, M. F. (1994). *A guide through college learning strategies* (2nd ed.). Dubuque, Iowa: Kendall/Hunt.

———. (1997). *It's all about choices: Why you do what you do . . . and other ways to do it.* Dubuque, Iowa: Kendall/Hunt.

Bogdan, R. & Biklen, S. K. (1992). *Qualitative research for education.* 2nd ed. Boston: Allyn and Bacon.

Braddock, II, J. H. & McPartland, J. M. (1988). Some cost and benefit considerations for black college students attending predominantly White versus predominantly black universities. In Michael T. Nettles (Ed.) *Toward black undergraduate student equality in American highereducation.* New York: Greenwood.

Bruno, E. M. (1990). *Follow-up study on guidance 7, college success students at Columbia College, 1989–90.* Columbia College, CA: Northern California Community Colleges Research Group. (ERIC Document Reproduction Service No. 332 734)

Clark S. B. & Crawford, S. L. (1992). An analysis of African-American first year college student attitudes and attrition rates. *Urban Education, 27*(1), 59–79.

Cross, T. & Slater, R.B. (1997). The commanding wealth advantage of college bound white students. *The Journal of Blacks in Higher Education, 15*–18, 80–90.

D'Augelli, A. R. & Hashberger, S. L. (1993). African American undergraduates on a predominantly white campus: Academic factors, social networks and campus climate. *Journal of Negro Education, 62*(1), 67–81.

Davis, J. E. (1994). College in black and white: Campus environment and academic achievement of African American males. *Journal of Negro Education, 63*(4), 620–633.

Dubois, W. E. B. (1989/1903). *The souls of black folk.* New York: Penguin.

Feagin, J. R., Vera, H., & Imani, N. (1996). *The agony of education: Black students at white colleges and universities.* New York: Routledge.

Fidler, P. P. & Hunter, M. S. (1989). How seminars enhance student success. In M. Lee Upcraft, John N. Gardner & Associates, *The freshmen year experience: Helping students survive and succeed in college* (198–215). San Francisco: Jossey-Bass.

Fleming, J. (1984). *Blacks in college.* San Francisco: Jossey-Bass.

———. (1983). Black women in black and white college environments: The making of a matriarch. *Journal of Social Issues, 39*(3), 41–54.

Gebelt, J. L., Parilis, G. M. Kramer, D. A., & Wilson, P. (1996). Retention at a large university: Combining skills with course content. *Journal of Developmental Education, 20*(1), 2–10.

Giles-Gee, H. F. (1989). Increasing the retention of black students: A multi-method approach. *Journal of College Student Development, 30*(3), 196–200.

Goldblatt, E. C. (1995). *'Round my way: Authority and double-consciousness in three urban high school writers.* Pittsburgh: University of Pittsburgh Press.

Green, M. F. (1989). Undergraduate students. *Minorities on campus: A handbook for enhancing diversity.* (pp. 29–54). Washington, D. C.: American Council on Education.

Hale, Janice E. (1994). *Unbank the fire: Visions for the education of African American children.* Baltimore: The John Hopkins University Press.

hooks, bell (1994). *Teaching to transgress: Education as the practice of freedom.* New York: Routledge.

Hynds, S. (1997). *On the brink: Negotiating literature and life with adolescents.* New York: Teachers College Press.

Jacobi, M. (1991). Mentoring and undergraduate academic success: A literature review. *Review of Educational Review, 61*(4), 505–532.

Jewler, A. J. (1989). Elements of an effective seminar: The university 101 program. In M. Lee Upcraft, John N. Gardner & Associates, *The freshmen year experience: Helping students survive and succeed in college* (198–215). San Francisco: Jossey-Bass.

Johnson, C. A. (1998). On becoming motivated to learn: The perceptions of students' learning experiences at a private northeastern university. Unpublished research apprenticeship report. Syracuse, NY: Syracuse University.

Kravitz, D. A. & Platania, J. (1993). Attitudes and beliefs about affirmative action: Effects of target and of respondent sex and ethnicity. *Journal of Applied Psychology, 78(6),* 928–938.

Levine, A. (1989). Who are today's freshmen? In M. Lee Upcraft, John N. Gardner & Associates, *The freshmen year experience: Helping Students survive and succeed in college* (15–24). San Francisco: Jossey-Bass.

Lewis, J. J. (1986). The black freshman network. *College and University, 61,* 135–140.

Love B. (1993). Issues and problems in the retention of black students in predominantly white institutions of higher education. *Equity and Excellence in Education, 26(1),* 27–35.

Mack, D. E., Tucker, T. W., Archuleta, R., DeGroot, G., Hernandez, A. A., & Cha, S. O. (1997). Interethnic relations on campus: Can't we all get along? *Journal of Multicultural Counseling and Development, 25,* 256–268.

Malaney, G. D. & Shively M. (1995). Academic and social expectations and experiences of first-year students of color. *NASPA Journal, 33(1),* 3–18.

Martin, O.L. & Williams-Dixon, R. (1991, June). The student-institutional fit for the African American student: Do college retention programs facilitate academic and social access? Paper presented at the Annual National Conference on Racial and Ethnic Relations in American Higher Education, San Antonio, TX.

McCauley, D. P. (1988). Effects of specific factors on blacks' persistence at a predominantly white university. *Journal of College Student Development,* 48–51.

Merriam, S. B. (1988). *Case study research in education: A qualitative approach.* San Francisco: Jossey-Bass.

Morrison, Toni (1972). *The bluest eye.* New York: Holt, Rinehart and Winston.

Nottingham, C. R., Rosen, D. H., & Parks, C. (1992). Psychological well being among African American university students. *Journal of College Student Development, 33,* 356–362.

O'Brien, E. M. (1989). Keeping them coming back for more: Retention personnel help schools hold on to minority students. *Black Issues in Higher Education, 5(22),* 2–5.

Ogbu, J. U. (1995). Literacy and black Americans: Comparative perspectives. In V. Gadsden & D. Wagner (Eds.), *Literacy among African-American youth: Issues in learning, teaching, and schooling* (pp. 83–100). Cresskill, NJ: Hampton Press.

Padilla, R. V., Trevino, J., Gonzalez, K., & Trevino, J. (1997). Developing local models of minority students' success in college. *Journal of College Student Development, 38(2),* 125–135.

Patton, M. Q. (1980). *Qualitative evaluation methods.* Beverly Hills: Sage.

Phelon-Rucker, M. L. (2000). African-American students' academic experience at a predominantly white institution: A critical-Interpretive approach to assessing organizational climate. Unpublished doctoral dissertation, Purdue University, West Lafayette, IN.

Phillip, M. C. (1993). Too many institutions still taking band-aid approach to minority student retention, experts say. *Black Issues in Higher Education, 9*(24), 24–28.

Pintrich, P. R. (1995). Understanding self-regulated learning. *New Directions for Teaching and Learning, 63,* 3–12.

Pobwajlo, M. (1989, October). The afy program at unhm: Reaching out to underprepared students. Paper presented at the meeting of the Annual Northeast Regional Conference on English in the Two Year college, Albany, NY.

Pounds, A. W. (1987). Black students' needs on predominantly white campuses. In D. J. Wright (Ed,) *Responding to the needs of today's minority students* (pp.23–38). San Francisco: Jossey-Bass.

———. (1989). Black students. In M. Lee Upcraft, John N. Gardner & Associates, *The freshmen year experience: Helping students survive and succeed in college* (277–286). San Francisco: Jossey-Bass.

Reis, E. (1989). *College success course, fall, 1988.* Palos Hills, IL: Moraine Valley Community College. (ERIC Document Reproduction Service No. 356 004)

Richardson, R. C., Jr., Simmons, H., & de los Santos, A. G., Jr. (1987). Graduating minority students: Lessons from ten success stories. *Change, 19,* (3), 20–27.

Rowser, J. F. (1997). Do African American students' perceptions of their needs have implications for retention? *Journal of Black Studies, 27*(5), 718–726.

Sax, L. J. & Arredondo, M. (1996). *Student attitudes toward affirmative action in higher education: Findings from a national study.* Paper presented at the meeting of the American Educational Research Association, New York, NY.

Selvam, A. (1999, April 20). Protesters win apology. *The Daily Orange: Syracuse University's Student Newspaper*, pp. 1, 4.

Shakur, Assata (1987). *Assata: An autobiography.* Westport, Connecticut: Lawrence Hill and Company.

Sheridan, E. M. (1982). Traditional skills for nontraditional students. *Improving College and University Teaching, 30,* 138–148.

Slater, R. B. (1995, Spring). Trends in black enrollment in higher education. *The Journal of Blacks in Higher Education, 7,* 7.

Smedley, B. D., Myers, H. F., & Harrell, S. P. (1993). Minority-status stresses and the college adjustment of ethnic minority freshmen. *Journal of Higher Education, 64*(4), 343–471.

Spitzberg, I. J., Jr. & Thorndike, V. V. (1992). *Creating community on college campuses.* Albany: State University Press of New York.

Steele, C. M. (1992). Race and the schooling of black Americans. *The Atlantic Monthly, 269* (4), 68–78.

Stupka, E. (1988, July). A position paper on making the case for student success course: The importance of front-loading the learning experience. Paper presented at the meeting of the National Conference on Student Retention, Boston, MA.

———. (1993). *An evaluation of the short term and long term impact a student success course has on academic performance and persistence.* Sacramento, CA: Sacramento City College. (ERIC Document Reproduction Service No. ED 364–300).

Syracuse University. *Chancellor's Task Force on Student Retention* (1997). Syracuse, New York.

Syracuse University. *Division of Student Support and Retention.* (1999). Syracuse Academic Improvement Program [Brochure]. Syracuse, New York.

Syracuse University Facts and Figures [On line]. Enrollment by ethnicity and level— fall enrollment for total university—1998–99. Available Internet: http://sumweb .syr.edu/ir/en_eth99.htm

The inclusive environment: A new environment for higher education. (1993). Washington, DC: Joint Center for Political and Economic Studies.

Thomas, G. E., & Hirsch, D. J. (1989). Blacks. In Levine, A. & Associates, *Shaping Higher Education's Future: Demographics Realities and Opportunities, 1990– 2000* (62–87). San Francisco: Jossey Bass.

Tinto, V. (1987). *Leaving college: Rethinking the causes and cures of student attrition.* Chicago: The University of Chicago Press.

Tinto, V. (1993). *Leaving college: Rethinking the causes and cures of student attrition* (2nd ed.). Chicago: The University of Chicago Press.

Townsend, L. (1994). How universities successfully retain and graduate black students. *The Journal of Blacks in Higher Education, 3–6* (4), 85–89.

Turner, C. S. V. (1994). Guests in someone else's house: Students of color. *The Review of Higher Education, 17* (4), 355–370.

Van Gennep, A. (1960). *The rites of passage.* Translated by M. Vizedon & G. Caffee. Chicago: University of Chicago Press. Originally published as Les rites de passage. Paris: Nourry, 1909.

Walters, E. (1996). Embracing the spirit of multiculturalism in higher education as a means of Black and Hispanic student retention. *Equity and Excellence in Education*, 29(3), 43–47.

Willie, C. V. & McCord, A. S. (1972). *Black students at white colleges.* New York: Praeger.

Wright, D. (1986). Misrepresenting the black student experience again: A rejoinder. *Student Personnel, 27*(3), 206–209.

———. (1987). Minority students: Developmental beginnings. In D. J. Wright (Ed.), *Responding to the needs of today's minority students*, (pp. 5–23). San Francisco: Jossey-Bass.

Zimmerman, B. J. (1990). Self-regulated learning and academic achievement: An overview. *Educational Psychologist, 25*(1), 3–17.

Index

About the Author

Cherlyn A. Johnson received her Ph.D. in English Education from Syracuse University and is currently an assistant professor of English at Virginia State University. Her areas of interest are multicultural education, study skills, and retention. She has been listed in Who's Who Among America's Teachers in the 2002, 2003–2004, and 2004–2005 editions.